Interactive Question Answering Workshop 2006

Held at HLT/NAACL 2006

New York, New York, USA
8-9 June 2006

ISBN: 978-1-61738-491-2

Printed from e-media with permission by:

Curran Associates, Inc.
57 Morehouse Lane
Red Hook, NY 12571
www.proceedings.com

Some format issues inherent in the e-media version may also appear in this print version.

Printed by Curran Associates, Inc. (2010)

Association for Computational Linguistics
209 N. Eighth Street
Stroudsburg, Pennsylvania 18360

Phone: 1-570-476-8006
Fax: 1-570-476-0860

acl@aclweb.org

Introduction

Welcome to the Interactive Question Answering Workshop at HLT-NAACL 2006.

In moving from factoid Question Answering (QA) to answering complex questions, it has become apparent that insufficient attention has been paid to the user's role in the process, other than as a source of one-shot factual questions or at best a sequence of related questions. Users both want to, and can do, a lot more: With respect to answers, users can usually disambiguate between a range of possible factoid answers and/or navigate information clusters in an answer space; In the QA process itself, users want to ask a wider range of question types, and respond to the system's answer in more ways than with another factual question. In short, real users demand real-time interactive question and answer capabilities, with coherent targeted answers presented in context for easy inspection. Repeat users will require user models that treat information already provided as background to novel information that is now available.

Such developments move the paradigm of QA away from single question, single answer modalities, toward interactive QA, where the system may retain memory of the QA process, and where users develop their understanding of a situation through an interactive QA dialogue. Dialogue systems already allow users to interact with simple, structured data such as train or flight timetables, using a dialogue component based on variations of finite-state models. These models make intensive use of the structure of the domain to constrain the range of possible interactions.

The goal of this two day workshop is to explore the area of dialogue as applied to the QA scenario, to extend current technology beyond factoid QA. We would like the workshop to produce some tangible output, which at the very least will be a blueprint for future development of the field. Each of the keynote speakers will add something to the discussion about the future direction (or past developments) of interactive QA. During these presentations, and the presentations of the participants, notes will be taken about research priorities, existing systems, methodologies and principles. At the end of the workshop, there will be a discussion section to produce a roadmap for the future development of interactive QA systems. This roadmap will be circulated to participants after the event.

Given the busy timetable of workshops and conferences around the world, we had an impresive number of submissions for IQA, allowing us to select only those papers which we felt made a real contribution towards the goal of this workshop. We hope you all enjoy the event and are able to actively participate in the discussions, and ultimately the creation of the roadmap for future research and development of Interactive Question Answering systems.

Nick Webb, June 2006.

Organizers:

Roberto Basili, University of Rome, Tor Vergata (ITALY)
Oliver Lemon, University of Edinburgh (UK)
Nick Webb, SUNY, Albany (USA) - Chair
Bonnie Webber, University of Edinburgh, (UK)

Program Committee:

John Donelan, AQUAINT Technical Steering Committee (USA)
Sanda Harabagiu, Language Computer Corporation (USA)
Ryuichiro Higashinaka, NTT (Japan)
Udo Kruschwitz, University of Essex (UK)
Steven Maiorano, AQUAINT Technical Steering Committee (USA)
Joe Polifroni, University of Sheffield (UK)
Sharon Small, SUNY, Albany (USA)
David Traum, ICT (USA)

Invited Speakers:

Jim Hieronymous, NASA
Tanya Korelsky, NSF
Heather McCallum-Bayliss, DTO
Tomek Strzalkowski, SUNY, Albany
Bill Woods, SUN Microsystems

Table of Contents

Conference Program

Thursday, June 8, 2006

9:00–9:30	Welcome, Introduction by Nick Webb
9:30–10:30	Invited Talk by Heather McCallum-Bayliss
10:30–11:00	Break
11:00–11:30	*Contextual Phenomena and Thematic Relations in Database QA Dialogues: Results from a Wizard-of-Oz Experiment* Núria Bertomeu, Hans Uszkoreit, Anette Frank, Hans-Ulrich Krieger and Brigitte Jörg
11:30–12:00	*WoZ Simulation of Interactive Question Answering* Tsuneaki Kato, Jun'ichi Fukumoto, Fumito Masui and Noriko Kando
12:00–12:30	Summary and Discussion: User's Role in QA: What Can They Do, What Should We Model? (Chair: Nick Webb)
12:30–14:00	Lunch
14:00–15:00	Invited Talk by Jim Hieronymous
15:00–15:30	*Modeling Reference Interviews as a Basis for Improving Automatic QA Systems* Nancy J. McCracken, Anne R. Diekema, Grant Ingersoll, Sarah C. Harwell, Eileen E. Allen, Ozgur Yilmazel and Elizabeth D. Liddy
15:30–16:00	Break
16:00–16:30	*Enhanced Interactive Question-Answering with Conditional Random Fields* Andrew Hickl and Sanda Harabagiu
16:30–17:00	Summary and Discussion: Domain Modeling: How Much Can We/Should We Capture? (Chair: TBA)

Friday, June 9, 2006

9:00–9:05	Welcome, Day One Summary by Nick Webb
9:05–9:30	Invited Talk byTanya Korelsky
9:30–10:30	Invited Talk by Bill Woods
10:30–11:00	Break
11:00–11:30	*A Data Driven Approach to Relevancy Recognition for Contextual Question Answering* Fan Yang, Junlan Feng and Giuseppe Di Fabbrizio
11:30–12:00	*Answering Questions of Information Access Dialogue (IAD) Task Using Ellipsis Handling of Follow-Up Questions* Jun'ichi Fukumoto
12:00–12:30	Summary and Discussion: IQA vs. IR (and Relevance Feedback) vs. Dialogue Systems (Chair: Tomek Strzalkowski)
12:30–14:00	Lunch
14:00–15:00	Invited Talk by Tomek Strzalkowski
15:00–15:30	*User-Centered Evaluation of Interactive Question Answering Systems* Diane Kelly, Paul Kantor, Emile Morse, Jean Scholtz and Ying Sun
15:30–16:00	Break
16:00–16:30	Summary and Discussion: Evaluation of IQA, Subjective vs. Objective? (Chair: TBA)
16:30–17:30	Roadmap Construction (Chair: Nick Webb)

Contextual phenomena and thematic relations in database QA dialogues: results from a Wizard-of-Oz Experiment

Núria Bertomeu, Hans Uszkoreit
Saarland University
Saarbrücken, Germany
uszkoreit|bertomeu@coli.uni-sb.de

Anette Frank, Hans-Ulrich Krieger and Brigitte Jörg
German Research Center of Artificial Intelligence
Saarbrücken, Germany
frank|krieger|joerg@dfki.de

Abstract

Considering data obtained from a corpus of database QA dialogues, we address the nature of the discourse structure needed to resolve the several kinds of contextual phenomena found in our corpus. We look at the thematic relations holding between questions and the preceding context and discuss to which extent thematic relatedness plays a role in discourse structure.

1 Introduction

As pointed out by several authors (Kato et al., 2004), (Chai and Ron, 2004), the information needs of users interacting with QA systems often go beyond a single stand-alone question. Often users want to research about a particular topic or event or solve a specific task. In such interactions we can expect that the individual user questions will be thematically connected, giving the users the possibility of reusing part of the context when formulating new questions.

That users implicitly refer to and even omit material which can be recovered from the context has already been replicated in several Wizard-of-Oz experiments simulating natural language interfaces to databases, (Carbonell, 1983), (Dahlbäck and Jönsson, 1989), the most frequent contextual phenomena being ellipsis, anaphora and definite descriptions.

A big challenge for interactive QA systems is, thus, the resolution of contextual phenomena. In order to be able to do so a system has to keep track of the user's focus of attention as the interaction proceeds. The attentional state at a given point in the interaction is given by the discourse structure. An open issue, however, is the nature of the discourse structure model needed in a QA system. Ahrenberg et al. (1990) argue that the discourse structure in NL interfaces is, given the limited set of actions to be performed by the system and the user, simpler than the one underlying human-human dialogue. Upon Ahrenberg et al. (1990) this is given by the discourse goals, rather than the overall goals of the user, as is the case in task-oriented dialogues, (Grosz and Sidner, 1986). Following Ahrenberg et al. (1990), the QA discourse is structured in segments composed by a pair of initiative-response units, like question-answer, or question-assertion, in the absence of an answer. A segment can be embedded in another segment if it is composed by a clarification request and its corresponding answer. The local context of a segment is given by the immediately preceding segment. Upon Ahrenberg et al. (1990), the latter reliably limits up the search space for antecedents of anaphoric devices and ellipsis. However, as we will see, there are few cases where the antecedents of contextual phenomena are to be found beyond the immediately preceding segments. This suggests that a more complex approach to discourse structure for QA systems is needed.

In more recent studies of interactive QA special attention has been paid to the thematic relatedness of questions, (Chai and Ron, 2004), (Kato et al., 2004). Chai and Ron (2004) propose a discourse modeling for QA interactions in which they keep track of thematic transitions between questions. Although

Proceedings of the Interactive Question Answering Workshop at HLT-NAACL 2006, pages 1–8,
New York City, NY, USA. June 2006.

the applications of tracking thematic transitions between questions have not been investigated in depth, Sun and Chai (2006) report on an experiment which shows that the use of a model of topic transitions based on Centering Theory improves query expansion for context questions. However, these previous studies on the thematic relations between questions are not based on collections of interactive data, but on questions centered around a topic that were collected in non-interactive environments. This means that they do not consider the answers to the questions, to which following questions can be related.

This paper presents data on different kinds of contextual phenomena found in a corpus of written natural language QA exchanges between human users and a human agent representing an interactive information service. We address two issues: the kinds and frequencies of thematic relations holding between the user questions and the preceding context, on the one hand, and the location of antecedents for the different contextual phenomena, on the other. We also discuss the question whether thematic relations can contribute to determine discourse structure and, thus, to the resolution of the contextual phenomena.

In the next section we present our data collection and the aspects of the annotation scheme which are relevant to the current work. In section 3 we present data regarding the overall thematic cohesion of the QA sessions. In section 4 we report on data regarding the co-occurrence of discourse phenomena and thematic relations and the distance between the phenomena and their antecedents. Finally, we discuss our findings with regard to their relevance with respect to the nature of discourse structure.

2 Corpus and methodology

2.1 Experimental set-up

In order to obtain a corpus of natural QA interactions, we designed a Wizard-of-Oz experiment. The experiment was set up in such a way that the exchanges between users and information system would be as representative as possible for the interaction between users and QA systems. We chose an ontology database instead of a text based closed domain QA system, however, because in order to simulate a real system short time responses were needed.

30 subjects took part in the experiment, which consisted in solving a task by querying LT-WORLD, an ontology containing information about language technology[1], in English. The modality of interaction was typing through a chat-like interface.

Three different tasks were designed: two of them concentrated on information browsing, the other one on information gathering. In the first task subjects had to find three traineeships at three different projects in three different institutions each on a different topic, and obtain some information about the chosen projects, like a contact address, a description, etc. In the second task, subjects had to find three conferences in the winter term and three conferences in the summer term, each one on a different topic and they had to obtain some information on the chosen conferences such as deadline, place, date. etc. Finally, the third task consisted of finding information for writing a report on European language technology in the last ten years. To this end, subjects had to obtain quantitative information on patents, organizations, conferences, etc.

The Wizard was limited to very few types of responses. The main response was answering a question. In addition, she would provide intermediate information about the state of processing if the retrieval took too long. She could also make statements about the contents of the database when it did not contain the information asked for or when the user appeared confused about the structure of the domain. Finally, she could ask for clarification or more specificity when the question could not be understood. Yet the Wizard was not allowed to take the initiative by offering information that was not explicitely asked for. Thus all actions of the Wizard were directly dependent on those of the user.

As a result we obtained a corpus of 33 logs (30 plus 3 pilot experiments) containing 125.534 words in 2.534 turns, 1.174 of which are user turns.

2.2 Annotation scheme

The corpus received a multi-layer annotaton[2] consisting of five levels. The levels of turns and part-of-speech were automatically annotated. The level of turns records information about the speaker and time

[1] See http://www.lt-world.org.

[2] We employed the annotation tool MMAX2 developed at EML Research, Heidelberg.

stamp. For the other levels - the questions level, the utterances level, and the entities level - a specific annotation scheme was developed. For these, we only explain the aspects relevant for the present study.

2.2.1 Questions

This level was conceived to keep track of the questions asked by the user which correspond to queries to the database. With the aim of annotating thematic relatedness between questions we distinguished two main kinds of thematic relations: those holding between a question and a previous question, *quest(ion)-to-quest(ion)-rel(ation)*, and those holding between a question and a previous answer, *quest(ion)-to-answ(er)-rel(ation)*.

Quest-to-quest-rels can be of the following types:

- *refinement* if the current question asks for the same type of entity as some previous question, but the restricting conditions are different, asking, thus, for a subset, superset or disjoint set of the same class.

  (1) US: How many projects on language technologies are there right now?
  US: How many have been done in the past?

- *theme-entity* if the current question is about the same entity as some previous question.

  (2) US: Where will the conference take place?
  US: What is the dead-line for applicants?

- *theme-property* if the current question asks for the same property as the immediately preceding question but for another entity.

  (3) US: Dates of TALK project?
  US: Dates of DEREKO?

- *paraphrase* if the question is the rephrasing of some previous question.

- *overlap* if the content of a question is subsumed by the content of some previous question.

We distinguish the following *quest-to-answ-rels*:

- *refinement* if the current question asks for a subset of the entities given in the previous answer.

  (4) LT: 3810.
  US: How many of them do research on language technology?

- *theme* if the current question asks about an entity first introduced in some previous answer.

  (5) LT: Semaduct, ...
  US: What language technology topics does the Semaduct project investigate?

Although Chai and Jin (2004) only consider transitions among questions in dialogues about events, most of our relations have a correspondence with theirs. *Refinement* corresponds to their *constraint refinement*, *theme-property* to their *participant-shift*, and *theme-entity* to their *topic exploration*.

2.2.2 Utterances

Utterances are classified according to their speech-act: *question*, *answer*, *assertion*, or *request*. Our annotation of discourse structure is identical in spirit to the one proposed by Ahrenberg et al. (1990). A segment is opened with a user question to the database and is closed with its corresponding answer or an assertion by the system. Clarification requests and their corresponding answers form segments which are embedded in other segments. Requests to wait and assertions about the processing of a question are also embedded in the segment opened by the question.

Fragmentary utterances are annotated at this level. We distinguish between fragments with a full linguistic source, fragments with a partial source, and fragments showing a certain analogy with the source. The first group corresponds to fragments which are structurally identical to the source and can, thus, be resolved by substitution or extension.

(6) US: Are there any projects on spell checking in Europe in the year 2006?
US: And in the year 2005?

Fragments with a partial source implicitly refer to some entity previously introduced, but some inference must be done in order to resolve them.

(7) US: How is the contact for that project?
US: Homepage?

The last group is formed by fragments which show some kind of parallelism with the source but which cannot be resolved by substitution.

(8) US: Which conferences are offered in this winter term in the subject of English language?
US: Any conferences concerning linguistics in general?

2.2.3 Reference

We distinguish the following types of reference to entities: identity or co-reference, subset/superset and bridging.

Co-reference occurs when two or more expressions denote the same entity. Within this group we found the following types of implicit co-referring expressions which involve different degrees of explicitness: elided NPs, anaphoric and deictic pronouns, deictic NPs, and co-referent definite NPs. Elided NPs are optional arguments, that is, they don't need to be in the surface-form of the sentence, but are present in the semantic interpretation. In (9) there is an anaphoric pronoun and an elided NP both referring to the conference *Speech TEK West 2006*.

(9) US: *The Speech TEK West 2006*, when does *it* take place?
LT: 2006-03-30 - 2006-04-01.
US: Until when can I hand in a paper *[ ]*?

Bridging is a definite description which refers to an entity related to some entity in the focus of attention. The resolution of bridging requires some inference to be done in order to establish the connection between the two entities. In example (2) in subsection 2.2.1 there is an occurrence of bridging, where *the dead-line* is meant to be the dead-line of the conference currently under discussion.

Finally, subset/superset reference takes place when a linguistic expression denotes a subset or superset of the set of entities denoted by some previous linguistic expression. Subset/superset reference is sometimes expressed through two interesting contextual phenomena: nominal ellipsis[3], also called semantic ellipsis, and one-NPs[4]. Nominal ellipsis occurs within an NP and it is namely the noun what is missing and must be recovered from the context. Here follows an example:

(10) US: Show me ***the three most important***.

3 Thematic follow-up

When looking at the thematic relatedness of the questions it's striking how well structured the interactions are regarding thematic relatedness. From 1047 queries to the database, 948 (90.54%) follow-up on some previous question or answer, or both. Only 99 questions (9.46%) open a new topic. 725 questions (69.25% of the total, 76.48% of the connected questions) are related to other questions, 332 (31.71% of the total, 35.02% of the connected questions) are related to answers, and 109 (10.41% of the total, 11.49% of the connected questions) are connected to both questions and answers. These numbers don't say much about how well structured the discourse is, since the questions could be far away from the questions or answers they are related to. However, this is very seldom the case. In 60% of the cases where the questions are thematically connected, they immediately follow the question they are related to, that is, the two questions are consecutive[5]. In 16.56% of the cases the questions immediately follow the answer they are related to. 74.58% of the questions, thus, immediately follow up the question or/and answer they are thematically related to[6].

Table 1 shows the distribution of occurrences and distances in segments for each of the relations described in subsection 2.2.1. We found that the most frequent question-to-question relation is *theme-entity*, followed by the question-to-answer relation *theme*. As you can see, for all the relations except *theme*, most occurrences are between very close standing questions or questions and answers, most of them holding between consecutive questions or questions and answers. The occurrences of the relation *theme*, however, are distributed along a wide range of distances, 29.70% holding between questions and answers that are 2 and 14 turns away from

[3]Note, however, that nominal ellipsis does not necessarily always denote a subset, but sometimes it can denote a disjoint set, or just lexical material which is omitted.

[4]One-NPs are a very rare in our corpus, so we are not considering them in the present study.

[5]By consecutive we mean that there is no intervening query to the database between the two questions. This doesn't imply that there aren't several intervening utterances and turns.

[6]9 questions are consecutive to the question and answer they are related to, respectively, that's why the total percentage of related consecutive questions is not 76.56%.

	REF. Q.	THEME E. Q.	THEME P. Q.	PARA. Q.	OVERL. Q.	REF. A.	THEME A.
TOTAL	74 (7.80%)	338 (35.65%)	107 (11.29%)	174 (18.35%)	29 (3.06%)	29 (3.06%)	303 (31.96%)
1 SEGM.	88.73%	81.65%	100%	60.92%	78.57%	83.34%	46.39%
2 SEGM.	5.63%	1.86%	0%	8.09%	21.43%	13.33%	10.20%

Table 1: Occurrences of the different thematic relations

REL. / PHEN.	THEME E. Q.	THEME P. Q.	THEME A.	REF. Q.	REF. A.	CONNECTED	TOTAL
FRAGMENT	53 (54.08%)	17 (16.32%)	3 (3.06%)	21 (21.42%)	0	97 (85.08%)	114
BRIDGING	40 (74.07%)	0	3 (5.55%)	1 (1.85%)	0	54 (58.69%)	92
DEFINITE NP	26 (78.78%)	0	4 (12.21%)	2 (6.10%)	0	33 (66%)	50
DEICTIC NP	19 (51.35%)	0	13 (35.13%)	2 (5.40%)	1 (2.70%)	37 (78.72%)	47
ANAPHORIC PRON.	13 (39.39%)	2 (6.06%)	10 (30.30%)	0	5 (15.15%)	33 (39.75%)	83
DEICTIC PRON.	2 (75%)	0	1 (25%)	0	0	3 (25%)	12
ELIDED NP	9 (69.23%)	0	2 (15.38%)	0	0	13 (61.90%)	21
NOMINAL ELLIPSIS	0	1 (7.69%)	6 (46.15%)	1 (7.69%)	5 (38.46%)	13 (81.25%)	16

Table 2: Contextual phenomena and the thematic relations holding between the questions containing them and the questions or answers containing the antecedents.

each other. This is because often several entities are retrieved with a single query and addressed later on separately, obtaining all the information needed about each of them before turning to the next one. We found also quite long distances for paraphrases, which means that the user probably forgot that he had asked that question, since he could have also scrolled back.

These particular distributions of thematic relations seem to be dependent on the nature of the tasks. We found some differences across tasks: the information gathering task elicited more refinement, while the information browsing tasks gave rise to more theme relations. It is possible that in an interaction around an event or topic we may find additional kinds of thematic relations and different distributions. We also observed different strategies among the subjects. The most common was to ask everything about an entity before turning to the next one, but some subjects preferred to ask about the value of a property for all the entities under discussion before turning to the next property.

4 Contextual phenomena: distances and thematic relatedness

There are 1113 user utterances in our corpus, 409 of which exhibit some kind of discourse phenomenon, i.e., they are context-dependent in some way. This amounts to 36.16% of the user utterances, a proportion which is in the middle of those found in the several corpora analyzed by Dahlbäck and Jönsson (1989)[7]. The amount of context-dependent user utterances, as Dahlbäck and Jönsson (1989) already pointed out, as well as the distribution of the different relations among questions and answers explained above, may be dependent on the nature of the task attempted in the dialogue.

Table 2 shows the distribution of the most frequent thematic relations holding between the questions containing the contextual phenomena considered in our study and the questions or answers containing their antecedents. The rightmost column shows the number of occurrences of each of the contextual phenomena described in subsection 2.2.3. The second column on the right shows the number of occurrences in which the antecedent is located in some previous segment and the question containing the contextual phenomenon is related through a thematic relation to the question or answer containing the antecedent. The percentages shown for each phenomenon are out of the total number of its occurrences. The remaining columns show frequen-

[7]They found a high variance according to the kind of task carried out in the different dialogues. Dialogues from tasks where there was the possibility to order something contained a higher number of context-dependent user initiatives, up to 54.62%, while information browsing dialogues contained a smaller number of context-dependent user initiatives, 16.95% being the lowest amount found.

cies of co-occurrence for each of the phenomena and thematic relations. The percentages shown for each phenomenon are out of the total number of its connected occurrences.

For the majority of investigated phenomena we observe that most questions exhibiting them stand in a thematic relation to the question or answer containing the antecedent. Although there may be several intermediate turns, the related questions are almost always consecutive, that is, the segment containing the contextual phenomenon immediately follows the segment containing the antecedent. In the remainder of the cases, the contextual phenomenon and its antecedent are usually in the same segment.

However, this is not the case for deictic and anaphoric pronouns. In most cases their antecedents are in the same segment and even in the same utterance or just one utterance away. This suggests that pronouns are produced in a more local context than other phenomena and their antecedents are first to be looked for in the current segment.

For almost all the phenomena the most frequent relation holding between the question containing them and the question or answer containing the antecedent is the question-to-question relation *theme-entity*, followed by the question-to-answer relation *theme*. This is not surprising, since we refer back to entities because we keep speaking about them.

However, fragments and nominal ellipsis show a different distribution. Fragments are related to their sources through the question-to-question relations *theme-property* and *refinement*, as well. Regarding the distribution of relations across the three different types of fragments we distinguish in our study, we find that the relations *refinement* and *theme-property* only hold between fragments with a full source and fragments of type analogy, and their respective sources. On the other hand, practically all fragments with a partial-source stand in a *theme-entity* relation to their source. Questions containing nominal ellipsis are mostly related to the preceding answer both through the relations *theme* and *refinement*.

4.1 Antecedents beyond the boundaries of the immediately preceding segment

As we have seen, the antecedents of more implicit co-referring expressions, like pronouns, are very often in the same segment as the expressions. The antecedents of less explicit co-referring expressions, like deictic and definite NPs, are mostly in the immediately preceding segment, but also often in the same segment. About 50% are 2 utterances away, 20% between 3 and 5, although we find distances up to 41 utterances for definite NPs.

However, there is a small number (11) of cases in which the antecedents are found across the boundaries of the immediately preceding segment. This poses a challenge to systems since the context needed for recovering these antecedent is not as local. The following example is a case of split antecedents. The antecedent of the elided NP is to be found across the two immediately preceding questions. Moreover, as you can see, the Wizard is not sure about how to interpret the missing argument, which can be because of the split antecedents, but also because of the amount of time passed, and/or because one of the answers is still missing, that is, more than one segment is open at the same time.

(11) US: Which are the webpages for ***European Joint Conferences on Theory and Practice of Software and International Conference on Linguistic Evidence***?
LT: Please wait... (waiting time)
US: Which are the webpages for ***International Joint Conference on Neural Networks and Translating and the Computer 27***?
LT: http://www.complang.ac, ... (1st answer)
US: Up to which date is it possible to send a paper, an abstract ***[ ]***?
LT: http://uwb.edu/ijcnn05/, ... (2nd answer)
LT: For which conference?
US: For ***all of the conferences I got the webpages***.

In the following example the antecedent of the definite NP is also to be found beyond the boundaries of the immediately preceding segment.

(12) US: What is the homepage of ***the project***?
LT: http://dip.semanticweb.org
USER: What is the email address of Christoph Bussler?
LT: The database does not contain this information.
US: Where does ***the project*** take place?

Here the user asks about the email address of a person who was previously introduced in the discourse as the coordinator of the project under discussion and then keeps on referring to the project with a definite NP. The intervening question is somehow related to the project, but not directly. There is a topic shift, as defined by Chai and Jin (2004), where the main topic becomes an entity related to the entity the preceding question was about. However, this topic shift is only at a very local level, since the dialogue participants keep on speaking about the project, that is, the topic at a more general level keeps on being the same. We can speak here of thematic nesting, since the second question is about an entity introduced in relation to the entity in focus of attention in the first question, and the third question is again about the same entity as the first. The project has not completely left the focus, but has remained in secondary focus during the second segment, to become again the main focus in the third segment. It seems that as long as the entity to which the focus of attention has shifted is related to the entity previously in focus of attention, the latter still also remains within the focus of attention.

5 Conclusions

The possibility of using contextual phenomena is given by certain types of thematic relatedness - especially *theme-entity* and *theme*, for co-reference and bridging, and *refinement*, *theme-entity* and *theme-property*, for fragments -, and contiguity of questions. As we have seen, the immediately preceding segment is in most cases the upper limit of the search space for the last reference to the entity, or the elided material in fragments. The directions of the search for antecedents, however, can vary depending on the phenomena, since for more implicit referring expressions antecedents are usually to be found in the same segment, while for less implicit referring expressions they are to be found in the preceding one.

These data are in accordance with what Ahrenberg et al. (1990) predict in their model. Just to consider the immediately preceding segment as the upper limit of the search space for antecedents is enough and, thus, no tracking of thematic relations is needed to resolve discourse phenomena. However, there are occurrences of more explicit types of co-reference expressions, where the antecedent is beyond the immediately preceding segment. As we have observed, in these cases the intervening segment/s shift the focus of attention to an entity (maybe provided in some previous answer) closely related to the one in focus of attention in the preceding segment. It seems that as long as this relation exists, even if there are many segments in between[8], the first entity remains in focus of attention and can be referred to by an implicit deictic or definite NP without any additional retrieval cue. We can speak of thematic nesting of segments, which seems to be analogous to the intentional structure in task-oriented dialogues as in (Grosz and Sidner, 1986), also allowing for reference with implicit devices to entities in the superordinate segments after the subordinated ones have been closed. It seems, thus, that thematic structure, like the discourse goals, also imposes structure on the discourse.

These cases, although not numerous, suggest that a more complex discourse structure is needed for QA interactions than one simply based on the discourse goals. The local context is given by the discourse segments, which are determined by the discourse goals, but a less local context may encompass several segments. As we have seen, reference with implicit devices to entities in the less local context is still possible. What seems to determine this less local context is a unique theme, about which all the segments encompassed by the context directly or indirectly are. So, although it does not seem necessary to track all the thematic transitions between the segments, it seems necessary to categorize the segments as being about a particular more global theme.

In a system like the one we simulated, having specific tasks in mind and querying structured data, a possible approach to model this extended context, or focus of attention, would be in terms of frames. Every time a new entity is addressed a new frame is activated. The frame encompasses the entity itself and the properties holding of it and other entities, as well as those entities. This would already allow us to successfully resolve bridging and fragments with a partial source. If the focus of atten-

[8]We found up to five intervening segments, one of them being a subsegment.

tion then shifts to one of the related entities, the user demanding particular information about it, then its frame is activated, but the previous frame also remains somehow active, although to a lesser degree. As long as there is a connection between the entities being talked about and a frame is not explicitly closed, by switching to speak about a different entity of the same class, for example, frames remain somehow active and implicit references will be accommodated within the activation scope.

In principle, the closer the relation to the entity currently in focus, the higher the degree of activation of the related entities. Yet, there may be cases of ambiguity, where only inferences about the goals of the user may help to resolve the reference, as in (13):

(13) US: How is the contact for that project?
LT: daelem@uia.ua.ac.be
US: What is the institute?
LT: Centrum voor Nederlandse Taal en Spraak.
US: Homepage?

Here the property "Homepage" could be asked about the institution or the project, the institution being more active. However, the Wizard interpreted it as referring to the project without hesitation because she knew that subjects were interested in projects, not in organizations. In order to resolve the ambiguity, we would need a system customized for tasks or make inferences about the goals of the users based on the kind of information they've been asking for. Determining at which level of nesting some expression has to be interpreted may involve plan recognition.

However, for open domain systems not having a knowledge-base with structured data it may be much more difficult to keep track of the focus of attention beyond the strictly local context. For other kinds of interactions which don't have such a structured nature as our tasks, this may also be the case. For example, in the information browsing tasks in (Kato et al., 2004), there is not a global topic encompassing the whole interaction, but the information needs of the user are given by the information he is encountering as the interaction proceeds, that is, he is browsing the information in a free way, without having particular goals or particular pieces of information he wants to obtain in mind. In such cases it may be difficult to determine how long frames are active if the nesting goes very far, as well as making any inferences about the user's plans. However, it might also be the case, that in that kind of interactions no implicit referring expressions are used beyond the segmental level, because there is no such an extended context. In order to find out, a study with interactive data should be carried out.

Acknowledgements

The research reported here has been conducted in the projects QUETAL and COLLATE II funded by the German Ministry for Education and Research, grants no. 01IWC02 and 01INC02, respectively. We are also grateful to Bonnie Webber for her helpful comments on the contents of this paper.

References

Ahrenberg Lars, Dahlbäck Nils and Arne Jönsson 1990. *Discourse representation and discourse management for natural language interfaces.* Proceeding of the Second Nordic Conference on Text Comprehension in Man and Machine, Täby, Sweeden, 1990.

Jaime G. Carbonell. 1983. *Discourse pragmatics and ellipsis resolution in task-oriented natural language interfaces.* Proceedings of the 21st annual meeting on Association for Computational Linguistics, Cambridge, Massachusetts, 1983

Chai Joyce Y. and Ron Jin. 2004. *Discourse Status for Context Questions.* HLT-NAACL 2004 Workshop on Pragmatics in Question Answering (HLT-NAACL 2004) Boston, MA, USA, May 3-7, 2004

Dahlbäck Nils and Arne Jönsson. 1989. *Empirical Studies of Discourse Representations for Natural Language Interfaces.* Proceedings of the Fourth Conference of the European Chapter of the ACL (EACL'89), Manchester.

Grosz Barbara and Candance Sidner. 1986. *Attention, Intention and the Structure of Discourse.* Computational Linguistics 12(3): 175-204.

Kato Tsuneaki, Fukumoto Junichi, Masui Fumito and Noriko Kando. 2004. *Handling Information Access Dialogue through QA Technologies - A novel challenge for open-domain question answering.* HLT-NAACL 2004 Workshop on Pragmatics in Question Answering (HLT-NAACL 2004) Boston, MA, USA, May 3-7, 2004

Sun Mingyu and Joycie J. Chai. 2006. *Towards Intelligent QA Interfaces: Discourse Processing for Context Questions.* International Conference on Intelligent User Interfaces, Sydney, Australia, January 2006

WoZ Simulation of Interactive Question Answering

Tsuneaki Kato
The University of Tokyo
kato@boz.c.u-tokyo.ac.jp

Jun'ichi Fukumoto
Ritsumeikan University
fukumoto@media.ritsumei.ac.jp

Fumito Masui
Mie University
masui@ai.info.mie-u.ac.jp

Noriko Kando
National Institute of Informatics
kando@nii.ac.jp

Abstract

QACIAD (Question Answering Challenge for Information Access Dialogue) is an evaluation framework for measuring interactive question answering (QA) technologies. It assumes that users interactively collect information using a QA system for writing a report on a given topic and evaluates, among other things, the capabilities needed under such circumstances. This paper reports an experiment for examining the assumptions made by QACIAD. In this experiment, dialogues under the situation that QACIAD assumes are collected using WoZ (Wizard of Oz) simulating, which is frequently used for collecting dialogue data for designing speech dialogue systems, and then analyzed. The results indicate that the setting of QACIAD is real and appropriate and that one of the important capabilities for future interactive QA systems is providing cooperative and helpful responses.

1 Introduction

Open-domain question answering (QA) technologies allow users to ask a question using natural language and obtain the answer itself rather than a list of documents that contain the answer (Voorhees et al.2000). While early research in this field concentrated on answering factoid questions one by one in an isolated manner, recent research appears to be moving in several new directions. Using QA systems in an interactive environment is one of those directions. A context task was attempted in order to evaluate the systems' ability to track context for supporting interactive user sessions at TREC 2001 (Voorhees 2001). Since TREC 2004, questions in the task have been given as collections of questions related to common topics, rather than ones that are isolated and independent of each other (Voorhees 2004). It is important for researchers to recognize that such a cohesive manner is natural in QA, although the task itself is not intended for evaluating context processing abilities since, as it is given the common topic, sophisticated context processing is not needed.

Such a direction has also been envisaged as a research roadmap, in which QA systems become more sophisticated and can be used by professional reporters and information analysts (Burger et al.2001). At some stage of that sophistication, a young reporter writing an article on a specific topic will be able to translate the main issue into a set of simpler questions and pose those questions to the QA system.

Another research trend in interactive QA has been observed in several projects that are part of the ARDA AQUAINT program. These studies concern scenario-based QA, the aim of which is to handle non-factoid, explanatory, analytical questions posed by users with extensive background knowledge. Issues include managing clarification dialogues in order to disambiguate users' intentions and interests; and question decomposition to obtain simpler and more tractable questions (Small et al.2003)(Hickl et

Proceedings of the Interactive Question Answering Workshop at HLT-NAACL 2006, pages 9–16,
New York City, NY, USA. June 2006.

al.2004).

The nature of questions posed by users and patterns of interaction vary depending on the users who use a QA system and on the environments in which it is used (Liddy 2002). The user may be a young reporter, a trained analyst, or a common man without special training. Questions can be answered by simple names and facts, such as those handled in early TREC conferences (Chai et al.2004), or by short passages retrieved like some systems developed in the AQUAINT program do (Small et al.2003). The situation in which QA systems are supposed to be used is an important factor of the system design and the evaluation must take such a factor into account. QACIAD (Question Answering Challenge for Information Access Dialogue) is an objective and quantitative evaluation framework to measure the abilities of QA systems used interactively to participate in dialogues for accessing information (Kato et al.2004a)(Kato et al.2006). It assumes the situation in which users interactively collect information using a QA system for writing a report on a given topic and evaluates, among other things, the capabilities needed under such circumstances, i.e. proper interpretation of questions under a given dialogue context; in other words, context processing capabilities such as anaphora resolution and ellipses handling.

We are interested in examining the assumptions made by QACIAD, and conducted an experiment, in which the dialogues under the situation QACIAD assumes were simulated using the WoZ (Wizard of Oz) technique (Fraser et al.1991) and analyzed. In WoZ simulation, which is frequently used for collecting dialogue data for designing speech dialogue systems, dialogues that become possible when a system has been developed are simulated by a human, a WoZ, who plays the role of the system, as well as a subject who is not informed that a human is behaving as the system and plays the role of its user. Analyzing the characteristics of language expressions and pragmatic devices used by users, we confirm whether QACIAD is a proper framework for evaluating QA systems used in the situation it assumes. We also examine what functions will be needed for such QA systems by analyzing intelligent behavior of the WoZs.

2 QACIAD and the previous study

QACIAD was proposed by Kato et al. as a task of QAC, which is a series of challenges for evaluating QA technologies in Japanese (Kato et al.2004b). QAC covers factoid questions in the form of complete sentences with interrogative pronouns. Any answers to those questions should be names. Here, "names" means not only names of proper items including date expressions and monetary values (called "named entities"), but also common names such as those of species and body parts. Although the syntactical range of the names approximately corresponds to compound nouns, some of them, such as the titles of novels and movies, deviate from that range. The underlying document set consists of newspaper articles. Being given various open-domain questions, systems are requested to extract exact answers rather than text snippets that contain the answers, and to return the answer along with the newspaper article from which it was extracted. The article should guarantee the legitimacy of the answer to a given question.

In QACIAD, which assumes interactive use of QA systems, systems are requested to answer series of related questions. The series of questions and the answers to those questions comprise an information access dialogue. All questions except the first one of each series have some anaphoric expressions, which may be zero pronouns, while each question is in the range of those handled in QAC. Although the systems are supposed to participate in dialogue interactively, the interaction is only simulated; systems answer a series of questions in batch mode. Such a simulation may neglect the inherent dynamics of dialogue, as the dialogue evolution is fixed beforehand and therefore not something that the systems can control. It is, however, a practical compromise for an objective evaluation. Since all participants must answer the same set of questions in the same context, the results for the same test set are comparable with each other, and the test sets of the task are reusable by pooling the correct answers.

Systems are requested to return one list consisting of all and only correct answers. Since the number of correct answers differs for each question and is not given, a modified F measure is used for the evaluation, which takes into account both precision and recall.

Two types of series were included in the QACIAD, which correspond to two extremes of information access dialogue: a gathering type in which the user has a concrete objective such as writing a report and summary on a specific topic, and asks a system a series of questions related to that topic; and a browsing type in which the user does not have any fixed topic of interest. Although the QACIAD assumes that users are interactively collecting information on a given topic and the gathering-type dialogue mainly occurs under such circumstances, browsing-type series are included in the task based on the observation that even when focusing on information access dialogue for writing reports, the systems must handle focus shifts appearing in browsing-type series. The systems must identify the type of series, as it is not given, although they need not identify changes of series, as the boundary is given. The systems must not look ahead to questions following the one currently being handled. This restriction reflects the fact that the QACIAD is a simulation of interactive use of QA systems in dialogues.

Examples of series of QACIAD are shown in Figure 1. The original questions are in Japanese and the figure shows their direct translations.

The evaluation of QA technologies based on QACIAD were conducted twice in QAC2 and QAC3, which are a part of the NTCIR-4 and NTCIR-5 workshops[1], respectively (Kato et al.2004b)(Kato et al.2005). It was one of the three tasks of QAC2 and the only task of QAC3. On each occasion, several novel techniques were proposed for interactive QA.

Kato et al. conducted an experiment for confirming the reality and appropriateness of QACIAD, in which subjects were presented various topics and were requested to write down series of questions in Japanese to elicit information for a report on that topic (Kato et al.2004a)(Kato et al.2006). The report was supposed to describe facts on a given topic, rather than state opinions or prospects on the topic. The questions were restricted to wh-type questions, and a natural series of questions that may contain anaphoric expressions and ellipses was constructed. Analysis of the question series collected in such a manner showed that 58% to 75% of questions for writing reports could be answered by values or names; a wide range of reference expressions is observed in questions in such a situation; and sequences of questions are sometimes very complicated and include subdialogues and focus shifts. From these observations they concluded the reality and appropriateness of the QACIAD, and validated the needs of browsing-type series in the task.

Series 30002
What genre does the "Harry Potter" series belong to?
Who is the author?
Who are the main characters in the series?
When was the first book published?
What was its title?
How many books had been published by 2001?
How many languages has it been translated into?
How many copies have been sold in Japan?

Series 30004
When did Asahi breweries Ltd. start selling their low-malt beer?
What is the brand name?
How much did it cost?
What brands of low-malt beer were already on the market at that time?
Which company had the largest share?
How much low-malt beer was sold compared to regular beer?
Which company made it originally?

Series 30024
Where was Universal Studio Japan constructed?
What is the nearest train station?
Which actor attended the ribbon-cutting ceremony on the opening day?
Which movie that he featured in was released in the New Year season of 2001?
What movie starring Kevin Costner was released in the same season?
What was the subject matter of that movie?
What role did Costner play in that movie?

Figure 1: Examples of Series in QACIAD

One of the objectives of our experiment is to confirm these results in a more realistic situation. The previous experiment setting is far from the actual situations in which QA systems are used, in which subjects have to write down their questions without getting the answers. Using WoZ simulation, it is confirmed whether or not this difference affected the result. Moreover, observing the behavior of WoZs, the capabilities and functions needed for QA sys-

[1]The NTCIR Workshop is a series of evaluation workshops designed to enhance research in information access technologies including information retrieval, QA, text summarization, extraction, and so on (NTCIR 2006).

tems used in such a situation are investigated.

3 Setting

Referring to the headlines in Mainichi and Yomiuri newspapers from 2000 and 2001, we selected 101 topics, which included events, persons, and organizations. On each of those topics, a *summary* of between 800 and 1600 characters long and an *abstract* of around 100 characters long were constructed using a full text search system on the newspaper articles.[2] Four experts shared this preparation work. Twenty topics were selected from among the original 101 on the basis that enough information was gathered and compiled into the summary.[3] The topics consisted of 5 persons, 2 organizations, 7 events, 5 artifacts, and 1 syndrome, which include Mr. Colin Powell, Charles, Prince of Wales, An accident of a Russian nuclear-powerd submarine, Concorde, "Harry Potter", and Windows XP.

The four experts who shared the preparation work acted as a WoZ in the simulated QA systems, and each expert participated in dialogues on the topic for which she/he wrote the summary and abstract, and tried to answer questions from users using the summary, a full text search system, and her/his memory.

Six subjects participated in the experiment and 10 topics were assigned to each subject. That is, each topic was handled by three subjects. The subjects behaved as users of simulated QA systems. Presented with the topic and abstract, the subjects were directed to think about questions beforehand assuming that they had to write a report on that topic, and then they participated in an information access dialogue with the "QA system." The suggested number of questions for each topic was around 10.

The dialogues were conducted through keyboards and character displays. The subjects were told that the system could answer only simple factoid questions, and the WoZs were instructed not to answer complicated questions such as asking for reasons and opinions. No restrictions on the usage of language expressions were imposed but were left to the discretion of the WoZs, though canned phrases such as "Please wait a moment" and "Sorry, the answer could not be found" were prepared in advance. The WoZs were also instructed that they could clarify users' questions when they were ambiguous or vague, and that their answers should be simple but cooperative and helpful responses were not forbidden.

USR: What is the title of the first book of the "Harry Potter" series?
SYS: "Harry Potter and the Sorcerer's Stone."
USR: How many books were sold?
SYS: The Japanese translation sold 600 thousand copies in the first half year after its publication.
USR: Who is the author?
SYS: J. K. Rowling.
USR: Who are the main characters (in that series)?
SYS: Harry Potter, Ron Weasley, Hagrid and so on.
USR: What kind of person is Harry Potter?
SYS: A child with a wizard and a witch for parents.
USR: What is the plot?
SYS: It is an adventure story involving Harry Potter and his friends who enter a school for witchcraft and wizardry.
USR: How many people went to the movie?
SYS: In the US, box-office sales of the movie "Harry Potter and the Sorcerer's Stone" reached 188 million dollars in the first 10 days after release.

Figure 2: Example of dialogues collected

An example of the dialogues collected is shown in Figure 2. In the figure, SYS stands for utterances of the QA system simulated by a WoZ and USR represents that of the user, namely a subject. In the rest of the paper, these are referred to as system's utterances and user's utterances, respectively.

4 Coding and Results

Excluding meta-utterances for dialogue control such as "Please wait a moment" and "That's all," 620 pairs of utterances were collected, of which 22 system utterances were for clarification. Among the remaining 598 cases, the system gave some answers in 502 cases, and the other 94 utterances were negative responses: 86 utterances said that the answer could not found; 10 utterances said that the question was too complicated or that they could not answer such type of question.

4.1 Characteristics of questions and answers

The syntactic classification of user utterances and its distribution is shown in Table 1. The numbers in

[2] Those lengths of Japanese texts roughly correspond to 300 to 600 words and 40 words of English text, respectively.

[3] We prepared 101 topics to meet the additional needs of other experiments. It is absolutely not the case that only 20 out of 101 were acceptable for our experiments.

Table 1: Syntactic classification of user utterances

Syntactic form	
Wh-type Question	87.7% (544)
Yes-no Question	9.5% (59)
Imperative (Information request)	2.6% (16)
Declarative (Answer to clarification)	0.2% (1)

Table 2: Categorization of user utterances by subject

Asking about	
Who, Where, What	32.5% (201)
When	16.3% (101)
How much/many (for several types of numerical values)	16.8% (104)
Why	6.5% (40)
How (for procedures or situations)	17.0% (105)
Definitions, Descriptions, Explanations	10.8% (67)
Other (Multiple Whs)	0.2% (1)

Table 3: Categorization of user utterances by answer type

Answered in	
Numerical values	14.3% (72)
Date expressions	16.7% (84)
Proper names	22.1% (111)
Common names	8.8% (44)
Compound nouns except names	4.2% (21)
Noun phrases	6.2% (31)
Clauses, sentences, or texts	27.7% (139)

Table 4: Pragmatic phenomena observed

Type	
No reference expression	203
Pronouns	14
Zero pronouns	317
Definite noun phrases	104
Ellipses	1

parentheses are numbers of occurrences. In spite of the direction of using wh-type questions, more than 10% of utterances are yes-no questions and imperatives for requesting information. Most of the user responses to clarification questions from the system are rephrasing of the question concerned; only one response has a declarative form. Examples of rephrasing will be shown in section 4.3.

The classification of user questions and requests according to the subject asked or requested is shown in Table 2; the classification of system answers according to their syntactic and semantic categorization is shown in Table 3. In Table 2, the classification of yes-no questions was estimated based on the information provided in the helpful responses to those. The classification in Table 3 was conducted based on the syntactic and semantic form of the exact part of the answer itself rather than on whole utterances of the system. For example, the categorization of the system utterance "He was born on April 5, 1935," which is the answer to "When was Mr. Colin Powell born?" is not a sentence but a date expression.

4.2 Pragmatic phenomena

Japanese has four major types of anaphoric devices: pronouns, zero pronouns, definite noun phrases, and ellipses. Zero pronouns are very common in Japanese, in which pronouns are not apparent on the surface. As Japanese also has a completely different determiner system from English, the difference between definite and indefinite is not apparent on the surface, and definite noun phrases usually have the same form as generic noun phrases. Table 4 shows a summary of such pragmatic phenomena observed. The total number is more than 620 as some utterances contain more than one anaphoric expression. "How many crew members were in *the submarine* when *the accident* happened?" is an example of such a question with multiple anaphoric expressions.

Among 203 questions with no reference expression, 60 questions (30%) are the first one of a series of utterances on the same topic. The others are divided into two cases. In the first and major case, the current foci appear literally rather than in pronouns or definite noun phrases. The second case, which is relatively minor, is the beginning of and the resume from a subdialogue. For example, when a user himself resumed talking about Charles, Prince of Wales after a few questions about his children, the user used a literal expression like "Who is the long-term partner of *Charles, Prince of Wales*?"; after talking about the details of the accident, a user asked "What is the major characteristic of *Concorde*?"

Out of 437 reference expressions excluding ellipses in Table 4, 94 expressions (22%) refer to items other than the global topic. Moreover, 76 expressions of those (81%) are a sole reference expression in the utterance. The existence of questions without referring to the global topic, accompanied with the existence of some questions with no reference expression, means that the focus shifts in those dialogues, and then the local focus can differ from the global topic.

4.3 Clarifications

As mentioned above, only 22 clarification utterances were observed in the experiment. They are categorized into those asking about an ambiguous referent (13 utterances) and those asking about a vague question subject (9 utterances). Examples of each case are shown below.

Clarification asking about an ambiguous referent

USR: When was he [Mr. Colin Powell] installed as head of security of the United States?
SYS: December 6, 2000.
USR: Who was the president at that time?
SYS: Mr. George W. Bush.
USR: Which political party did he belong to?
SYS: *Whose political party are you asking about?*
USR: Which political party did Mr. Colin Powell belong to?

Clarification asking about a vague question subject

USR: Who developed Windows XP?
SYS: *Are you asking for a company name?*
USR: What company developed Windows XP?

4.4 Cooperative and helpful responses

Rather than simple and literal answers to the users' questions and requests, cooperative and helpful responses, in which, for example, information not requested directly by a user was additionally provided (Kaplan 1983), were observed frequently. The results of analyzing such cooperative and helpful behavior in the system responses are shown in Table 5. Questions asking reasons, procedures, situations, definitions, descriptions or explanations, which are categorized into the last three categories except others in Table 2, were excluded from this analysis, since for those questions it is difficult to judge objectively whether some information is additional or not and, in addition, most of those are out of the scope of QACIAD, which is our main interest. Table 5 shows the number of occurrences and its percentage among positive responses. Sometimes, more than one behavior was observed in one utterance. 148 utterances out of 334 positive responses (44%) contained some helpful behavior. The definitions and manually constructed examples of cooperative and helpful behavior listed in Table 5 are shown below.

Table 5: Cooperative and helpful behavior observed

Type of behavior	
Providing additional information	52 (15.6%)
Providing detailed information	38 (11.4%)
Elaboration of subject	38 (11.4%)
Providing alternative information	47 (14.1%)
Exemplification	28 (8.4%)
Providing speculations	3 (0.9%)

Providing additional information Information not requested directly from a user is additionally provided.

USR: What year was Mr. Colin Powell born?
SYS: He was born in 1935 in New York.

Providing detailed information More detailed information than that requested directly by a user is provided.

USR: What year was Mr. Colin Powell born?
SYS: He was born on April 5, 1935.

Elaboration of subject A relatively vague subject of a question is elaborated and made concrete. In the following example, a question with a vague expression, "how well" is answered by a value as a concrete statistic.

USR: How well did the movie do?
SYS: In the US, box-office sales reached 188 million dollars in the first 10 days after release.

Providing alternative information Rather than exact information a user requested, alternative related information is provided. An alternative may be proposed by relaxing the condition imposed by the user. In the following example, attendance figures were altered to box-office sales.

USR: How many people went to the movie?

SYS: In the US, box-office sales reached 188 million dollars in the first 10 days after release.

Exemplification Instead of a comprehensive list or abstracted general description, some major instances are listed.

USR: What kinds of character goods are on sale?

SYS: Stuffed owls, uniforms for schools of witchcraft and wizardry, and so on.

Providing speculation Rather than fact, speculations and opinions are provided, which can be considered a special case of providing alternative information. Although there are few cases of such behavior in Table 5, there were many such answers in response to questions asking for reasons and situations.

USR: What exploded?

SYS: It is surmised that torpedoes in the shed at the fore exploded.

Detecting and correcting erroneous user assumptions is a famous helpful behavior discussed in the literature (Pollack 1989) (Kaplan 1983). Only two occurrences of such behavior were observed, one of which is shown below.

USR: How long did it take from the explosion until the shipwreck?

SYS: The explosion happened while the submarine was going down, and ...

5 Discussion

The analysis of dialogue collected by the WoZ simulation showed very similar results to those obtained in a previous study, in which sequences of questions were written down by subjects without knowing the answers to questions. That is, as shown in Table 2, when users asked questions to get information for a report, the number of why-questions was relatively small. Moreover, there were fewer questions requesting an explanation or definition than expected, probably because definition questions such as "Who is Mr. Colin Powell?" were decomposed into relatively concrete questions such as those asking for his birthday and birthplace. The remainder (65%) could be answered in values and names. Table 3 indicates that 62% of the questions in our experiments were answered by values or names. If compound nouns describing events or situations, which are usually distinguished from names, are considered to be in the range of answers, the percentage of answerable questions reaches 68%. From these results, the setting of QACIAD looks realistic where users write reports interacting with a QA system handling factoid questions that have values and names as answers.

A wide range of reference expressions is observed in information access dialogues for writing reports. Moreover, our study confirmed that those sequences of questions were sometimes very complicated and included subdialogues and focus shifts. It is expected that using an interactive QA system that can manage those pragmatic phenomena will enable fluent information access dialogue for writing reports. In this sense, the objective of QACIAD is appropriate.

It could be concluded from these results that the reality and appropriateness of QACIAD was reconfirmed in a more realistic situation. And yet suspicion remains that even in our WoZ simulation, the subjects were not motivated appropriately, as suggested by the lack of dynamic dialogue development in the example shown in Figure 2. Especially, the users often gave up too easily when they did not obtain answers to prepared questions.[4] The truth, however, may be that in the environment of gathering information for writing reports, dynamic dialogue development is limited compared to the case when trained analysts use QA systems for problem solving. If so, research on this type of QA systems represents a proper milestone toward interactive QA systems in a broad sense.

Another finding of our experiment is the importance of cooperative and helpful responses. Nearly half of WoZ utterances were not simple literal responses but included some cooperative and helpful behavior. This situation contrasts with a relatively small number of clarification dialogues. The importance of this behavior, which was emphasized in research on dialogues systems in the 80s and 90s, was reconfirmed in the latest research, although question-answering technologies were redefined in the late 90s. Some behavior such as providing alternative information could be viewed as a second-best

[4] It is understandable, however, that there were few rephrasing attempts since users were informed that paraphrasing such as "What is the population of the US?" to "How many people are living in the US?" are usually in vain.

strategy of resource-bounded human WoZs. Even so, it is impossible to eliminate completely the need for such a strategy by improving core QA technologies. In addition, intrinsic cooperative and helpful behavior such as providing additional information was also often observed. These facts, accompanied by the fact that such dialogues are perceived as fluent and felicitous, suggest that the capability to behave cooperatively and helpfully is essential for interactive QA technologies.

6 Conclusion

Through WoZ simulation, the capabilities and functions needed for interactive QA systems used as a participant in information access dialogues for writing reports were examined. The results are compatible with those of previous research, and reconfirmed the reality and appropriateness of QACIAD. A new finding of our experiment is the importance of cooperative and helpful behavior of QA systems, which was frequently observed in utterances of the WoZs who simulated interactive QA systems. Designing such cooperative functions is indispensable. While this fact is well known in the context of past research on dialogue systems, it has been reconfirmed in the context of the latest interactive QA technologies.

References

Joyce Y. Chai and Rong Jin. 2004. Discource Structure for Context Question Answering. *Proceedings of HLT-NAACL2004 Workshop on Pragmatics of Question Answering*, pp. 23-30.

John Burger, Claire Cardie, Vinay Chaudhri, et al. 2001. Issues, Tasks and Program Structures to Roadmap Research in Question & Answering (Q&A) `http://www-nlpir.nist.gov/projrcts/duc/roadmpping.html`.

Norma M. Fraser and G. Nigel Gilbert. 1991. Simulating speech systems. *Computer Speech and Language*, Vol 5, No.1, pp. 81-99.

Andrew Hickl, Johm Lehmann, John Williams, and Sanda Harabagiu. 2004. Experiments with Interactive Question Answering in Complex Scenarios. *Proceedings of HLT-NAACL2004 Workshop on Pragmatics of Question Answering*, pp. 60-69.

Joerrold Kaplan. 1983. Cooperative Responses from a Portable Natural Language Database Query System. Michael Brady and Robert C. Berwick eds. *Computational Models of Discourse*, pp. 167–208, The MIT Press.

Tsuneaki Kato, Jun'ichi Fukumoto, Fumito Masui and Noriko Kando. 2004a. Handling Information Access Dialogue through QA Technologies – A novel challenge for open-domain question answering –. *Proceedings of HLT-NAACL2004 Workshop on Pragmatics of Question Answering*, pp. 70-77.

Tsuneaki Kato, Jun'ici Fukumoto and Fumito Masui. 2004b. Question Answering Challenge for Information Access Dialogue – Overview of NTCIR4 QAC2 Subtask 3 –. *Proceedings of NTCIR-4 Workshop Meeting*.

Tsuneaki Kato, Jun'ici Fukumoto and Fumito Masui. 2005. An Overview of NTCIR-5 QAC3. *Proceedings of Fifth NTCIR Workshop Meeting*, pp. 361–372.

Tsuneaki Kato, Jun'ici Fukumoto, Fumito Masui and Noriko Kando. 2006. Are Open-domain Question Answering Technologies Useful for Information Access Dialogues? – An empirical study and a proposal of a novel challenge – *ACL Trans. of Asian Language Information Processing*, In Printing.

Elizabeth D. Liddy. 2002. Why are People Asking these Questions? : A Call for Bringing *Situation* into Question-Answering System Evaluation. *LREC Workshop Proceedings on Question Answering · Strategy and Resources*, pp. 5-8.

NTCIR Project Home Page. 2006. `http://research.nii.ac.jp/~ntcadm/index-en.html`

Martha E. Pollack. 1989. Plans as Complex Mental Attitudes. Philip R. Cohen, Jerry Morgan and Martha E. Pollack eds. *Intentions in Communication*, pp. 77–103, The MIT Press.

Sharon Small, Nobuyuki Shimizu, Tomek Strzalkowski, and Liu Ting 2003. HITIQA: A Data Driven Approach to Interactive Question Answering: A Preliminary Report *AAAI 2003 Spring Symposium New Directions in Question Answering*, pp. 94-104.

Ellen M. Voorhees and Dawn M. Tice. 2000. Building a Question Answering Test Collection *the Proceedings of the 23rd Annual International ACM SIGIR Conference on Research and Development in Information Retrieval*, pp. 200 - 207.

Ellen M. Voorhees. 2001. Overview of the TREC 2001 Question Answering Track. *Proceedings of TREC 2001*.

Ellen M. Voorhees. 2004. Overview of the TREC 2004 Question Answering Track. *Proceedings of TREC 2004*.

Modeling Reference Interviews as a Basis for Improving Automatic QA Systems

Nancy J. McCracken, Anne R. Diekema, Grant Ingersoll, Sarah C. Harwell, Eileen E. Allen, Ozgur Yilmazel, Elizabeth D. Liddy
Center for Natural Language Processing
Syracuse University
Syracuse, NY 13244
{ njmccrac, diekemar, gsingers, scharwel, eeallen, oyilmaz, liddy}@syr.edu

Abstract

The automatic QA system described in this paper uses a reference interview model to allow the user to guide and contribute to the QA process. A set of system capabilities was designed and implemented that defines how the user's contributions can help improve the system. These include tools, called the Query Template Builder and the Knowledge Base Builder, that tailor the document processing and QA system to a particular domain by allowing a Subject Matter Expert to contribute to the query representation and to the domain knowledge. During the QA process, the system can interact with the user to improve query terminology by using Spell Checking, Answer Type verification, Expansions and Acronym Clarifications. The system also has capabilities that depend upon, and expand the user's history of interaction with the system, including a User Profile, Reference Resolution, and Question Similarity modules

1 Introduction

Reference librarians have successfully fielded questions of all types for years using the Reference Interview to clarify an unfocused question, narrow a broad question, and suggest further information that the user might not have thought to ask for. The reference interview tries to elicit sufficient information about the user's real need to enable a librarian to understand the question enough to begin searching. The question is clarified, made more specific, and contextualized with relevant detail. Real questions from real users are often "ill-formed' with respect to the information system; that is, they do not match the structure of 'expectations' of the system (Ross et al., 2002). A reference interview translates the user's question into a representation that the librarian and the library systems can interpret correctly. The human reference interview process provides an ideal, well-tested model of how questioner and answerer work together co-operatively and, we believe, can be successfully applied to the digital environment. The findings of researchers applying this model in online situations (Bates, 1989, Straw, 2004) have enabled us to understand how a system might work with the user to provide accurate and relevant answers to complex questions.

Our long term goal in developing Question-Answering (QA) systems for various user groups is to permit, and encourage users to positively contribute to the QA process, to more nearly mirror what occurs in the reference interview, and to develop an automatic QA system that provides fuller, more appropriate, individually tailored responses than has been available to date.

Building on our Natural Language Processing (NLP) experience in a range of information access applications, we have focused our QA work in two areas: 1) modeling the subject domain of the collections of interest to a set of

Proceedings of the Interactive Question Answering Workshop at HLT-NAACL 2006, pages 17–24,
New York City, NY, USA. June 2006.

users for whom we are developing the QA system, and; 2) modeling the query clarification and negotiation interaction between the information seeker and the information provider. Examples of these implementation environments are:

1. Undergraduate aerospace engineering students working in collaborative teams on course projects designing reusable launch vehicles, who use a QA system in their course-related research.
2. Customers of online business sites who use a QA system to learn more about the products or services provided by the company, or who wish to resolve issues concerning products or service delivery.

In this paper, we describe the capabilities we have developed for these specific projects in order to explicate a more general picture of how we model and utilize both the domains of inquiry and typical interaction processes observed in these diverse user groups.

2 Background and related research

Our work in this paper is based on two premises: 1) user questions and responsive answers need to be understood within a larger model of the user's information needs and requirements, and, 2) a good interactive QA system facilitates a dialogue with its users to ensure it understands and satisfies these information needs. The first premise is based on the long-tested and successful model of the reference interview (Bates, 1997, Straw, 2004), which was again validated by the findings of an ARDA-sponsored workshop to increase the research community's understanding of the information seeking needs and cognitive processes of intelligence analysts (Liddy, 2003). The second premise instantiates this model within the digital and distributed information environment.

Interactive QA assumes an interaction between the human and the computer, typically through a combination of a clarification dialogue and user modeling to capture previous interactions of users with the system. De Boni et al. (2005) view the clarification dialogue mainly as the presence or absence of a relationship between the question from the user and the answer provided by the system. For example, a user may ask a question, receive an answer and ask another question in order to clarify the meaning, or, the user may ask an additional question which expands on the previous answer. In their research De Boni et al. (2005) try to determine automatically whether or not there exists a relationship between a current question and preceding questions, and if there is a relationship, they use this additional information in order to determine the correct answer.

We prefer to view the clarification dialogue as more two-sided, where the system and the user actually enter a dialogue, similar to the reference interview as carried out by reference librarians (Diekema et al., 2004). The traditional reference interview is a cyclical process in which the questioner poses their question, the librarian (or the system) questions the questioner, then locates the answer based on information provided by the questioner, and returns an answer to the user who then determines whether this has satisfied their information need or whether further clarification or further questions are needed. The HITIQA system's (Small et al., 2004) view of a clarification system is closely related to ours—their dialogue aligns the understanding of the question between system and user. Their research describes three types of dialogue strategies: 1) narrowing the dialogue, 2) broadening the dialogue, and 3) a fact seeking dialogue.

Similar research was carried out by Hori et al. (2003), although their *system* automatically determines whether there is a need for a dialogue, not the *user*. The system identifies ambiguous questions (i.e. questions to which the system could not find an answer). By gathering additional information, the researchers believe that the system can find answers to these questions. Clarifying questions are automatically generated based on the ambiguous question to solicit additional information from the user. This process is completely automated and based on templates that generate the questions. Still, removing the cognitive burden from the user through automation is not easy to implement and can be the cause of error or misunderstanding. Increasing user involvement may help to reduce this error.

As described above, it can be seen that interactive QA systems have various levels of dialogue automation ranging from fully automatic (De Boni et al., 2004, Hori et al., 2004) to a strong user involvement (Small et al., 2004, Diekema et al., 2004). Some research suggests that clarification dialogues in open-domain systems are more unpredictable than those in restricted domain systems, the latter lending itself better to automation (Hori et al., 2003, Jönsson et al., 2004). Incorporating the user's inherent knowledge of the intention of their query is quite feasible in restricted domain systems and should improve the quality of answers returned, and make the experience of the user a less frustrating one. While many of the systems described above are promising in terms of IQA, we believe that incorporating knowledge of the user in the question negotiation dialogue is key to developing a more accurate and satisfying QA system.

3 System Capabilities

In order to increase the contribution of users to our question answering system, we expanded our traditional domain independent QA system by adding new capabilities that support system-user interaction.

3.1 Domain Independent QA

Our traditional domain-independent QA capability functions in two stages, the first information retrieval stage selecting a set of candidate documents, the second stage doing the answer finding within the filtered set. The answer finding process draws on models of question types and document-based knowledge to seek answers without additional feedback from the user. Again, drawing on the modeling of questions as they interact with the domain representation, the system returns answers of variable lengths on the fly in response to the nature of the question since factoid questions may be answered with a short answer, but complex questions often require longer answers. In addition, since our QA projects were based on closed collections, and since closed collections may not provide enough redundancy to allow for short answers to be returned, the variable length answer capability assists in finding answers to factoid questions. The QA system provides answers in the form of short answers, sentences, and answer-providing passages, as well as links to the full answer-providing documents. The user can provide relevance feedback by selecting the full documents that offer the best information. Using this feedback, the system can reformulate the question and look for a better set of documents from which to find an answer to the question. Multiple answers can be returned, giving the user a more complete picture of the information held within the collection.

One of our first tactics to assist in both question and domain modeling for specific user needs was to develop tools for Subject Matter Experts (SMEs) to tailor our QA systems to a particular domain. Of particular interest to the interactive QA community is the Query Template Builder (QTB) and the Knowledge Base Builder (KBB).

Both tools allow a priori alterations to question and domain modeling for a community, but are not sensitive to *particular* users. Then the interactive QA system permits question- and user-specific tailoring of system behavior simply because it allows subject matter experts to change the way the system understands their need at the time of the search.

Question Template Builder (QTB) allows a subject matter expert to fine tune a question representation by adding or removing stopwords on a question-by-question basis, adding or masking expansions, or changing the answer focus. The QTB displays a list of Question-Answer types, allows the addition of new Answer Types, and allows users to select the expected answer type for specific questions. For example, the subject matter expert may want to adjust particular "who" questions as to whether the expected answer type is "person" or "organization". The QTB enables organizations to identify questions for which they want human intervention and to build specialized term expansion sets for terms in the collection. They can also adjust the stop word list, and refine and build the Frequently or Previously Asked Question (FAQ/PAQ) collection.

Knowledge Base Builder (KBB) is a suite of tools developed for both commercial and government customers. It allows the users to view and extract terminology that resides in their document collections. It provides useful statistics about the corpus that may indicate portions that require attention in customization. It collects frequent / important terms with categorizations to enable ontology building (semi-automatic, permitting human review), term collocation for use in identifying which sense of a word is used in the collection for use in term expansion and categorization review. KBB allows companies to tailor the QA system to the domain vocabulary and important concept types for their market. Users are able to customize their QA applications through human-assisted automatic procedures. The Knowledge Bases built with the tools are

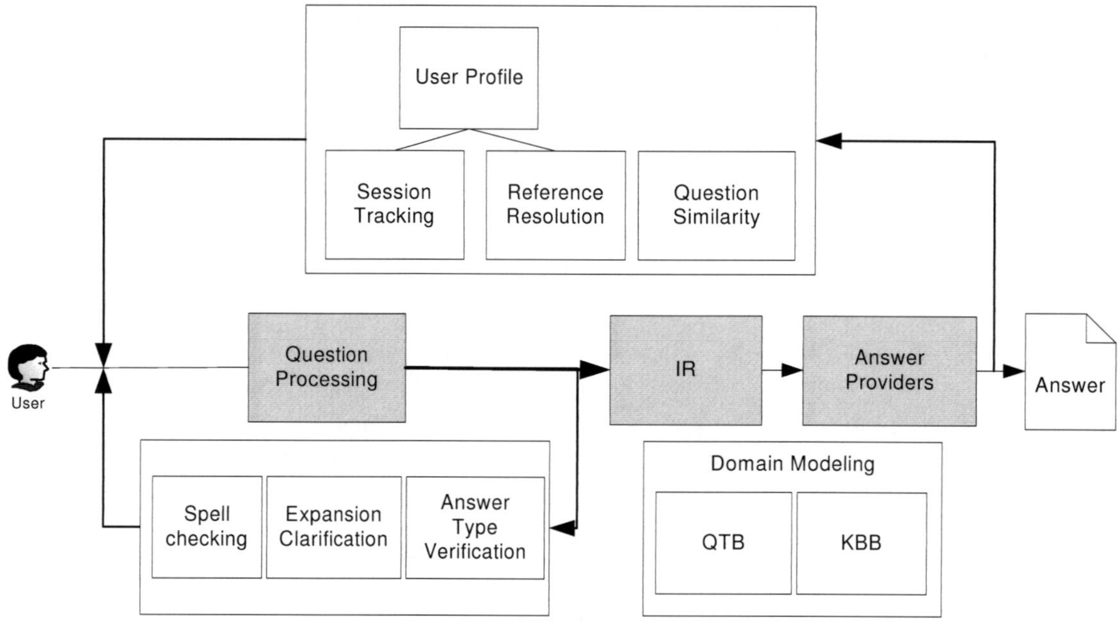

Figure 1. System overview

primarily lexical semantic taxonomic resources. These are used by the system in creating frame representations of the text. Using automatically harvested data, customers can review and alter categorization of names and entities and expand the underlying category taxonomy to the domain of interest. For example, in the NASA QA system, experts added categories like "material", "fuel", "spacecraft" and "RLV", (Reusable Launch Vehicles). They also could specify that "RLV" is a subcategory of "spacecraft" and that space shuttles like "Atlantis" have category "RLV". The KBB works in tandem with the QTB, where the user can find terms in either documents or example queries

3.2 Interactive QA Development

In our current NASA phase, developed for undergraduate aerospace engineering students to quickly find information in the course of their studies on reusable launch vehicles, the user can view immediate results, thus bypassing the Reference Interviewer, or they may take the opportunity to utilize its increased functionality and interact with the QA system. The capabilities we have developed, represented by modules added to the system, fall into two groups. Group One includes capabilities that draw on direct interaction with the user to clarify what is being asked and that address terminological issues. It includes Spell Checking, Expansion Clarification, and Answer Type Verification. Answers change dynamically as the user provides more input about what was meant. Group Two capabilities are dependent upon, and expand upon the user's history of interaction with the system and include User Profile, Session Tracking, Reference Resolution, Question Similarity and User Frustration Recognition modules. These gather knowledge about the user, help provide co-reference resolution within an extended dialogue, and monitor the level of frustration a user is experiencing.

The capabilities are explained in greater detail below. Figure 1 captures the NASA system process and flow.

Group One:

In this group of interactive capabilities, after the user asks a query, answers are returned as in a typical system. If the answers presented aren't satisfactory, the system will embark on a series of interactive steps (described below) in which alternative spelling, answertypes, clarifications and expansions will be suggested. The user can choose from the system's suggestions or type in their own. The system will then revise the query and return a new set of answers. If those answers aren't satisfactory, the user can continue interacting with the system until appropriate answers are found.

Spell checking: Terms not found in the index of the document collection are displayed as potentially misspelled words. In this preliminary phase, spelling is checked and users have the opportunity to select correct and/or alternative spellings.

AnswerType verification: The interactive QA system displays the type of answer that the system is looking for in order to answer the question. For example for the question, *Who piloted the first space shuttle?,* the answer type is 'person', and the system will limit the search for candidate short answers in the collection to those that are a person's name. The user can either accept the system's understanding of the question or reject the type it suggests. This is particularly useful in semantically ambiguous questions such as "Who makes Mountain Dew?" where the system might interpret the question as needing a person, but the questioner actually wants the name of a company.

Expansion: This capability allows users to review the possible relevant terms (synonyms and group members) that could enhance the question-answering process. The user can either select or deselect terms of interest which do or do not express the intent of the question. For example, if the user asks: *How will aerobraking change the orbit size?* then the system can bring back the following expansions for "aerobraking": *By aerobraking do you mean the following: 1) aeroassist, 2) aerocapture, 3) aeromaneuvering, 4) interplanetary transfer orbits, or 5) transfer orbits.*

Acronym Clarification: For abbreviations or acronyms within a query, the full explications known by the system for the term can be displayed back to the user. The clarifications implemented are a priori limited to those that are relevant to the domain. In the aerospace domain for example, if the question was *What is used for the TPS of the RLV?,* the clarifications of TPS would be *thermal protection system, thermal protection subsystem, test preparation sheet*, or *twisted pair shielded*, and the clarification of RLV would be *reusable launch vehicle.* The appropriate clarifications can be selected to assist in improving the search. For a more generic domain, the system would offer broader choices. For example, if the user types in the question: *What educational programs does the AIAA offer?,* then the system might return: *By AIAA, do you mean (a) American Institute of Aeronautics and Astronautics (b) Australia Indonesia Arts Alliance or (c) Americans for International Aid & Adoption?*

Group Two:

User Profile: The User Profile keeps track of more permanent information about the user. The profile includes a small standard set of user attributes, such as the user's name and / or research interests. In our commercially funded work, selected information gleaned from the question about the user was also captured in the profile. For example, if a user asks "How much protein should my husband be getting every day?", the fact that the user is married can be added to their profile for future marketing, or for a new line of dialogue to ask his name or age. This information is then made available as context information for the QA system to resolve references that the user makes to themselves and their own attributes.

For the NASA question-answering capability, to assist students in organizing their questions and results, there is an area for users to save their searches as standing queries, along with the results of searching (Davidson, 2006). This information, representing topics and areas of interest, can help to focus answer finding for new questions the user asks.

Not yet implemented, but of interest, is the ability to save information such as a user's preferences (format, reliability, sources), that could be used as filters in the answer finding process.

Reference Resolution: A basic feature of an interactive QA system is the requirement to understand the user's questions and responsive answers as one session. The sequence of questions and answers forms a natural language dialogue between the user and the system. This necessitates NLP processing at the discourse level, a primary task of which is to resolve references across the session. Building on previous work in this area done for the Context Track of TREC 2001 (Harabagiu et al, 2001) and additional work (Chai and Jin, 2004) suggesting discourse structures are needed to understand the question/answer sequence, we have developed session-based reference resolution capability. In a dialogue, the user naturally includes referring phrases that require several types of resolution.

The simplest case is that of referring pronouns, where the user is asking a follow-up question, for example:

Q1: When did Madonna enter the music business?
A1: Madonna's first album, Madonna, came out in 1983 and since then she's had a string of hits, been a major influence in the music industry and become an international icon.
Q2: When did she first move to NYC?

In this question sequence, the second question contains a pronoun, "she", that refers to the person "Madonna" mentioned both in the previous question and its answer. Reference resolution would transform the question into "When did Madonna first move to NYC?"

Another type of referring phrase is the definite common noun phrase, as seen in the next example:

Q1: If my doctor wants me to take Acyclovir, is it expensive?
A1: Glaxo-Wellcome, Inc., the company that makes Acyclovir, has a program to assist individuals that have HIV and Herpes.
Q2: Does this company have other assistance programs?

The second question has a definite noun phrase "this company" that refers to "Glaxo-Wellcome, Inc." in the previous answer, thus transforming the question to "Does Glaxo-Wellcome, Inc. have other assistance programs?"

Currently, we capture a log of the question/answer interaction, and the reference resolution capability will resolve any references in the current question that it can by using linguistic techniques on the discourse of the current session. This is almost the same as the narrative coreference resolution used in documents, with the addition of the need to understand first and second person pronouns from the dialogue context. The coreference resolution algorithm is based on standard linguistic discourse processing techniques where referring phrases and candidate resolvents are analyzed along a set of features that typically includes gender, animacy, number, person and the distance between the referring phrase and the candidate resolvent.

Question Similarity: Question Similarity is the task of identifying when two or more questions are related. Previous studies (Boydell et al., 2005, Balfe and Smyth, 2005) on information retrieval have shown that using previously asked questions to enhance the current question is often useful for improving results among like-minded users. Identifying related questions is useful for finding matches to Frequently Asked Questions (FAQs) and Previously Asked Questions (PAQs) as well as detecting when a user is failing to find adequate answers and may be getting frustrated. Furthermore, similar questions can be used during the reference interview process to present questions that other users with similar information needs have used and any answers that they considered useful.

CNLP's question similarity capability comprises a suite of algorithms designed to identify when two or more questions are related. The system works by analyzing each query using our Language-to-Logic (L2L) module to identify and weight keywords in the query, provide expansions and clarifications, as well as determine the focus of the question and the type of answer the user is expecting (Liddy et al., 2003). We then compute a series of similarity measures on two or more L2L queries. Our measures adopt a variety of approaches, including those that are based on keywords in the query: cosine similarity, keyword string matching, expansion analysis, and spelling variations. In addition, two measures are based on the representation of the whole query:answer type and answer frame analysis. An answer frame is our representation of the meaningful extractions contained in the query, along with metadata about where they occur and any other extractions that relate to in the query.

Our system will then combine the weighted scores of two or more of these measures to determine a composite score for the two queries, giving more weight to a measure that testing has determined to be more useful for a particular task.

We have utilized our question similarity module for two main tasks. For FAQ/PAQ (call it XAQ) matching, we use question similarity to compare the incoming question with our database of XAQs. Through empirical testing, we determined a threshold above which we consider two questions to be similar.

Our other use of question similarity is in the area of frustration detection. The goal of frustration detection is to identify the signs a user may be giving that they are not finding relevant answers so that the system can intervene and offer alternatives before the user leaves the system, such as similar questions from other users that have been successful.

4 Implementations:

The refinements to our Question Answering system and the addition of interactive elements have been implemented in three different, but related working systems, one of which is strictly an enhanced IR system. None of the three incorporates all of these capabilities. In our work for MySentient, Ltd, we developed the session-based reference resolution capability, implemented the variable length and multiple answer capability, modified our processing to facilitate the building of a user profile, added FAQ/PAQ capability, and our Question Similarity capability for both FAQ/PAQ matching and frustration detection. A related project, funded by Syracuse Research Corporation, extended the user tools capability to include a User Interface for the KBB and basic processing technology. Our NASA project has seen several phases. As the project progressed, we added the relevant developed capabilities for improved performance. In the current phase, we are implementing the capabilities which draw on user choice.

5 Conclusions and Future Work

The reference interview has been implemented as an interactive dialogue between the system and the user, and the full system is near completion. We are currently working on two types of evaluation of our interactive QA capabilities. One is a system-based evaluation in the form of unit tests, the other is a user-based evaluation. The unit tests are designed to verify whether each module is working correctly and whether any changes to the system adversely affect results or performance. Crafting unit tests for complex questions has proved challenging, as no gold standard for this type of question has yet been created. As the data becomes available, this type of evaluation will be ongoing and part of regular system development.

As appropriate for this evolutionary work within specific domains for which there are not gold standard test sets, our evaluation of the QA systems has focused on qualitative assessments. What has been a particularly interesting outcome is what we have learned in elicitation from graduate students using the NASA QA system, namely that they have multiple dimensions on which they evaluate a QA system, not just traditional recall and precision (Liddy et al, 2004). The high level dimensions identified include system performance, answers, database content, display, and expectations. Therefore the evaluation criteria we believe appropriate for IQA systems are centered around the display (UI) category as described in Liddy et al, (2004). We will evaluate aspects of the UI input subcategory, including question understanding, information need understanding, querying style, and question formulation assistance. Based on this user evaluation the system will be improved and retested.

References

Evelyn Balfe and Barry Smyth. 2005. An Analysis of Query Similarity in Collaborative Web Search. In *Proceedings of the 27th European Conference on Information Retrieval*. Santiago de Compostela, Spain.

Marcia J. Bates. 1989. The Design of Browsing and Berrypicking Techniques for the Online Search Interface. *Online Review*, 13: 407-424.

Mary Ellen Bates. 1997. The Art of the Reference Interview. *Online World*. September 15.

Oisín Boydell, Barry Smyth, Cathal Gurrin, and Alan F. Smeaton. 2005. A Study of Selection Noise in Collaborative Web Search. In *Proceedings of the 19th International Joint Conference on Artificial Intelligence*. Edinburgh, Scotland. http://www.ijcai.org/papers/post-0214.pdf

Joyce Y. Chai, and Rong Jin. 2004. Discourse Structure for Context Question Answering. In *Proceedings of the Workshp on the Pragmatics of Quesiton Answering,* HST-NAACL, Boston. http://www.cse.msu.edu/~rongjin/publications/HLTQAWorkshop04.pdf

Barry D. Davidson. 2006. *An Advanced Interactive Discovery Learning Environment for Engineering Education: Final Report.* Submitted to R. E. Gillian, National Aeronautics and Space Administration.

Marco De Boni and Suresh Manandhar. 2005. Implementing Clarification Dialogues in Open Domain Question Answering. *Natural Language Engineering* 11(4): 343-361.

Anne R. Diekema, Ozgur Yilmazel, Jiangping Chen, Sarah Harwell, Lan He, and Elizabeth D. Liddy. 2004. Finding Answers to Complex Questions. In *New Directions in Question Answering*. (Ed.) Mark T. Maybury. The MIT Press, 141-152.

Sanda Harabagiu, Dan Moldovan, Marius Paşca, Mihai Surdeanu, Rada Mihalcea, Roxana Gîrju, Vasile Rus, Finley Lăcătuşu, Paul Morărescu, Răzvan Bunescu. 2001. Answering Complex, List and Context Questions with LCC's Question-Answering Server, TREC 2001.

Chiori Hori, Takaaki Hori., Hideki Isozaki, Eisaku Maeda, Shigeru Katagiri, and Sadaoki Furui. 2003. Deriving Disambiguous Queries in a Spoken Interactive ODQA System. In *ICASSP*. Hongkong, I: 624-627.

Arne Jönsson, Frida Andén, Lars Degerstedt, Annika Flycht-Eriksson, Magnus Merkel, and Sara Norberg. 2004. Experiences from Combining Dialogue System Development With Information Extraction Techniques. In *New Directions in Question Answering*. (Ed.) Mark T. Maybury. The MIT Press, 153-164.

Elizabeth D. Liddy. 2003. Question Answering in Contexts. Invited Keynote Speaker. ARDA AQUAINT Annual Meeting. Washington, DC. Dec 2-5, 2003.

Elizabeth D. Liddy, Anne R. Diekema, Jiangping Chen, Sarah Harwell, Ozgur Yilmazel, and Lan He. 2003. What do You Mean? Finding Answers to Complex Questions. *Proceedings of New Directions in Question Answering*. AAAI Spring Symposium, March 24-26.

Elizabeth D. Liddy, Anne R. Diekema, and Ozgur Yilmazel. 2004. Context-Based Question-Answering Evaluation. In *Proceedings of the 27th Annual ACM-SIGIR Conference.* Sheffield, England

Catherine S. Ross, Kirsti Nilsen, and Patricia Dewdney. 2002. *Conducting the Reference Interview.* Neal-Schuman, New York, NY.

Sharon Small, Tomek Strzalkowski, Ting Liu, Nobuyuki Shimizu, and Boris Yamrom. 2004. A Data Driven Approach to Interactive QA. In *New Directions in Question Answering*. (Ed.) Mark T. Maybury. The MIT Press, 129-140.

Joseph E. Straw. 2004. Expecting the Stars but Getting the Moon: Negotiating around Patron Expectations in the Digital Reference Environment. In *The Virtual Reference Experience: Integrating Theory into Practice.* Eds. R. David Lankes, Joseph Janes, Linda C. Smith, and Christina M. Finneran. Neal-Schuman, New York, NY.

Enhanced Interactive Question-Answering with Conditional Random Fields

Andrew Hickl and Sanda Harabagiu
Language Computer Corporation
Richardson, Texas 75080
andy@languagecomputer.com

Abstract

This paper describes a new methodology for enhancing the quality and relevance of suggestions provided to users of interactive Q/A systems. We show that by using Conditional Random Fields to combine relevance feedback gathered from users along with information derived from discourse structure and coherence, we can accurately identify irrelevant suggestions with nearly 90% F-measure.

1 Introduction

Today's interactive question-answering (Q/A) systems enable users to pose questions in the context of extended dialogues in order to obtain information relevant to complex research scenarios. When working with an interactive Q/A system, users formulate sequences of questions which they believe will return answers that will let them reach certain information goals.

Users need more than answers, however: while they might be cognizant of many of the different types of information that they need, few – if any – users are capable of identifying all of the questions that must be asked and answered for a particular scenario. In order to take full advantage of the Q/A capabilities of current systems, users need access to sources of domain-specific knowledge that will expose them to new concepts and ideas and will allow them to ask better questions.

In previous work (Hickl et al., 2004; Harabagiu et al., 2005a), we have argued that interactive question-answering systems should be based on a *predictive dialogue architecture* which can be used to provide users with both precise answers to their questions as well as suggestions of relevant research topics that could be explored throughout the course of an interactive Q/A dialogue.

Typically, the quality of interactive Q/A dialogues has been measured in three ways: (1) efficiency, defined as the number of questions that the user must pose to find particular information, (2) effectiveness, defined by the relevance of the answer returned, and (3) user satisfaction (Scholtz and Morse, 2003).

In our experiments with an interactive Q/A system, (known as FERRET), we found that performance in each of these areas improves as users are provided with suggestions that are relevant to their domain of interest. In FERRET, suggestions are made to users in the form of predictive question-answer pairs (known as QUABs) which are either generated automatically from the set of documents returned for a query (using techniques first described in (Harabagiu et al., 2005a)), or are selected from a large database of questions-answer pairs created offline (prior to a dialogue) by human annotators.

Figure 1 presents an example of ten QUABs that were returned by FERRET in response to the question *"How are EU countries responding to the worldwide increase of job outsourcing to India?"*.

While FERRET's QUABs are intended to provide users with relevant information about a domain of interest, we can see from Figure 1 that users do not always agree on which QUAB suggestions are relevant. For example, while someone unfamiliar to the notion of "job outsourcing" could benefit from

Proceedings of the Interactive Question Answering Workshop at HLT-NAACL 2006, pages 25–32,
New York City, NY, USA. June 2006.

Relevant?		QUAB Question
$User_1$	$User_2$	
NO	YES	$QUAB_1$: What EU countries are outsourcing jobs to India?
YES	YES	$QUAB_2$: What EU countries have made public statements against outsourcing jobs to India?
NO	YES	$QUAB_3$: What is job outsourcing?
YES	YES	$QUAB_4$: Why are EU companies outsourcing jobs to India?
NO	NO	$QUAB_5$: What measures has the U.S. Congress taken to stem the tide of job outsourcing to India?
YES	NO	$QUAB_6$: How could the anti-globalization movements in EU countries impact the likelihood that the EU Parliament will take steps to prevent job outsourcing to India?
YES	YES	$QUAB_7$: Which sectors of the EU economy could be most affected by job outsourcing?
YES	YES	$QUAB_8$: How has public opinion changed in the EU on job outsourcing issues over the past 10 years?
YES	YES	$QUAB_9$: What statements has French President Jacques Chirac made about job outsourcing?
YES	YES	$QUAB_{10}$: How has the EU been affected by anti-job outsourcing sentiments in the U.S.?

Figure 1: Examples of QUABs.

a QUAB like $QUAB_3$: "*What is job outsourcing?*", we expect that a more experienced researcher would find this definition to be uninformative and potentially irrelevant to his or her particular information needs. In contrast, a complex QUAB like $QUAB_6$: "*How could the anti-globalization movements in EU countries impact the likelihood that the EU Parliament will take steps to prevent job outsourcing to India?*" could provide a domain expert with relevant information, but would not provide enough background information to satisfy a novice user who might not be able to interpret this information in the appropriate context.

In this paper, we present results of a new set of experiments that seek to combine feedback gathered from users with a relevance classifier based on conditional random fields (CRF) in order to provide suggestions to users that are not only related to the topic of their interactive Q/A dialogue, but provide them with the new types of information they need to know.

Section 2 presents the functionality of several of FERRET's modules and describes the NLP techniques for processing questions as well as the framework for acquiring domain knowledge. In Section 3 we present two case studies that highlight the impact of user background. Section 4 describes a new class of user interaction models for interactive Q/A and presents details of our CRF-based classifier. Section 5 presents results from experiments which demonstrate that user modeling can enhance the quality of suggestions provided to both expert and novice users. Section 6 summarizes the conclusions.

2 The FERRET Interactive Question-Answering System

We believe that the quality of interactions produced by an interactive Q/A system can be enhanced by predicting the range of questions that a user might ask while researching a particular topic. By providing suggestions from a large database of question-answer pairs related to a user's particular area of interest, interactive Q/A systems can help users gather the information they need most – without the need for complex, mixed-initiative clarification dialogues.

FERRET uses a large collection of QUAB question-answer pairs in order to provide users with suggestions of new research topics that could be explored over the course of a dialogue. For example, when a user asks a question like *What is the result of the European debate on outsourcing to India?* (as illustrated in (Q1) in Table 1), FERRET returns a set of answers (including (A1) and proposes the questions in (Q2), (Q3), and (Q4) as suggestions of possible continuations of the dialogue. Users then have the freedom to choose how the dialogue should be continued, either by (1) ignoring the suggestions made by the system, (2) selecting one of the proposed QUAB questions and examining its associated answer, or (3) resubmitting the text of the QUAB question to FERRET's automatic Q/A system in order to retrieve a brand-new set of answers.

(Q1) What is the result of the European debate on outsourcing to India?
(A1) Supporters of economic openness understand how outsourcing can strengthen the competitiveness of European companies, as well as benefi t jobs and growth in India.
(Q2) Has the number of customer service jobs outsourced to India increased since 1990?
(Q3) How many telecom jobs were outsourced to India from EU-based companies in the last 10 years?
(Q4) Which European Union countries have experienced the most job losses due to outsourcing over the past 10 years?

Table 1: Sample Q/A Dialogue.

FERRET was designed to evaluate how databases of topic-relevant suggestions could be used to enhance the overall quality of Q/A dialogues. Figure 2 illustrates the architecture of the FERRET system. Questions submitted to FERRET are initially processed by a *dialogue shell* which (1) decomposes complex questions into sets of simpler questions (using techniques first described in (Harabagiu et al., 2005a)), (2) establishes discourse-level relations between the current question and the set of questions

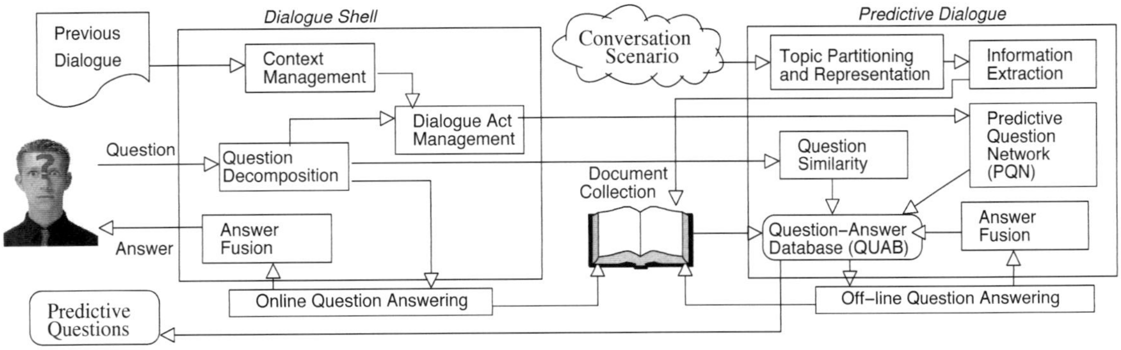

Figure 2: FERRET - A Predictive Interactive Question-Answering Architecture.

already entered into the discourse, and (3) identifies a set of basic dialogue acts that are used to manage the overall course of the interaction with a user.

Output from FERRET's dialogue shell is sent to an *automatic question-answering system* which is used to find answers to the user's question(s). FERRET uses a version of LCC's PALANTIR question-answering system (Harabagiu et al., 2005b) in order to provide answers to questions in documents. Before being returned to users, answer passages are submitted to an *answer fusion* module, which filters redundant answers and combines answers with compatible information content into single coherent answers.

Questions and relational information extracted by the *dialogue shell* are also sent to a *predictive dialogue* module, which identifies the QUABs that best meet the user's expected information requirements. At the core of the FERRET's *predictive dialogue* module is the *Predictive Dialogue Network* (PQN), a large database of QUABs that were either generated off-line by human annotators or created on-line by FERRET (either during the current dialogue or during some previous dialogue)[1]. In order to generate QUABs automatically, documents identified from FERRET's automatic Q/A system are first submitted to a *Topic Representation* module, which computes both topic signatures (Lin and Hovy, 2000) and enhanced topic signatures (Harabagiu, 2004) in order to identify a set of topic-relevant passages. Passages are then submitted to an *Information Extraction* module, which annotates texts with a wide range of lexical, semantic, and syntactic information, including (1) morphological information, (2) named entity information from LCC's CICEROLITE named entity recognition system, (3) semantic dependencies extracted from LCC's PropBank-style semantic parser, and (4) syntactic parse information. Passages are then transformed into natural language questions using a set of question formation heuristics; the resultant QUABs are then stored in the PQN. Since we believe that the same set of relations that hold between questions in a dialogue should also hold between pairs of individual questions taken in isolation, discourse relations are discovered between each newly-generated QUAB and the set of QUABs stored in the PQN. FERRET's *Question Similarity* module then uses the similarity function described in (Harabagiu et al., 2005a) – along with relational information stored in the PQN – in order to identify the QUABs that represent the most informative possible continuations of the dialogue. QUABs are then ranked in terms of their relevance to the user's submitted question and returned to the user.

3 Two Types of Users of Interactive Q/A Systems

In order to return answers that are responsive to users' information needs, interactive Q/A systems need to be sensitive to the different questioning strategies that users employ over the course of a dialogue. Since users gathering information on the same topic can have significantly different information needs, interactive Q/A systems need to be able to accommodate a wide range of question types in order to help users find the specific information that

[1]Techniques used by human annotators for creating QUABs were first described in (Hickl et al., 2004); full details of FERRET's automatic QUAB generation components are provided in (Harabagiu et al., 2005a).

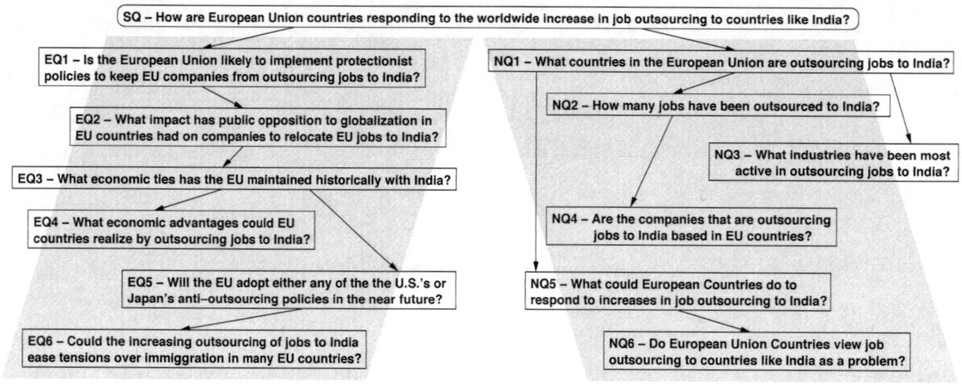

Figure 3: Expert User Interactions Versus Novice User Interactions with a Q/A System.

they are looking for.

In past experiments with users of interactive Q/A systems (Hickl et al., 2004), we have found that a user's access to sources of domain-specific knowledge significantly affects the types of questions that a user is likely to submit to a Q/A system. Users participate in information-seeking dialogues with Q/A systems in order to learn "new" things – that is, to acquire information that they do not currently possess. Users initiate a set of speech acts which allow them to maximize the amount of new information they obtain from the system while simultaneously minimizing the amount of redundant (or previously-acquired) information they encounter. Our experiments have shown that Q/A systems need to be sensitive to two kinds of users: (1) expert users, who interact with a system based on a working knowledge of the conceptual structure of a domain, and (2) novice users, who are presumed to have limited to no foreknowledge of the concepts associated with the domain. We have found that novice users that possess little or no familiarity with a domain employ markedly different questioning strategies than expert users who possess extensive knowledge of a domain: while novices focus their attention in queries that will allow them to discover basic domain concepts, experts spend their time asking questions that enable them to evaluate their hypotheses in the context of a the currently available information. The experts tend to ask questions that refer to the more abstract domain concepts or the complex relations between concepts. In a similar fashion, we have discovered that users who have access to structured sources of domain-specific knowledge (e.g. knowledge bases, conceptual networks or ontologies, or mixed-initiative dialogues) can end up employing more "expert-like" questioning strategies, despite the amount of domain-specific knowledge they possess.

In real-world settings, the knowledge that expert users possess enables them to formulate a set of hypotheses – or belief states – that correspond to each of their perceived information needs at a given moment in the dialogue context. As can be seen in the dialogues presented in Figure 3, expert users generally formulate questions which seek to validate these belief states in the context of a document collection. Given the global information need in S_1, it seems reasonable to presume that questions like EQ_1 and EQ_2 are motivated by a user's expectation that *protectionist policies or* public opposition to globalization could impact a European Union country's willingness to take steps to stem job outsourcing to India. Likewise, questions like EQ_5 are designed to provide the user with information that can decide between two competing belief states: in this case, the user wants to know whether the European Union is more likely to model the United States or Japan in its policies towards job outsourcing. In contrast, without a pre-existing body of domain-specific knowledge to derive reasonable hypotheses from, novice users ask questions that enable them to discover the concepts (and the relations between concepts) needed to formulate new, more specific hypotheses and questions. Returning again to Figure 3, we can see that questions like NQ_1 and NQ_3 are designed to discover new knowledge that the user does not currently possess, while questions like NQ_6 try to establish whether or not the user's hypothesis (i.e. namely, that EU countries view job outsourcing to India as an problem) is valid and deserves further consideration.

4 User Interaction Models for Relevance Estimation

Unlike systems that utilize mixed initiative dialogues in order to determine a user's information needs (Small and Strzalkowski, 2004), systems (like FERRET) which rely on interactions based on predictive questioning have traditionally not incorporated techniques that allow them to gather relevance feedback from users. In this section, we describe how we have used a new set of user interaction models (UIM) in conjunction with a relevance classifier based on conditional random fields (CRF) (McCallum, 2003; Sha and Pereira, 2003) in order to improve the relevance of the QUAB suggestions that FERRET returns in response to a user's query.

We believe that systems based on predictive questioning can derive feedback from users in three ways. First, systems can learn which suggestions or answers are relevant to a user's domain of interest by tracking which elements users select throughout the course of a dialogue. With FERRET, each answer or suggestion presented to a user is associated with a hyperlink that links to the original text that the answer or QUAB was derived from. While users do not always follow links associated with passages they deem to be relevant to their query, we expect that the set of selected elements are generally more likely to be relevant to the user's interests than unselected elements. Second, since interactive Q/A systems are often used to gather information for inclusion in written reports, systems can identify relevant content by tracking the text passages that users copy to other applications, such as text editors or word processors. Finally, predictive Q/A systems can gather explicit feedback from users through the graphical user interface itself. In a recent version of FERRET, we experimented with adding a "relevance checkbox" to each answer or QUAB element presented to a user; users were then asked to provide feedback to the system by selecting the checkboxes associated with answers that they deemed to be particularly relevant to the topic they were researching.

4.1 User Interaction Models

We have experimented with three models that we have used to gather feedback from users of FERRET. The models are illustrated in Figure 4.

UIM_1:	Under this model, the set of QUABs that users copied from were selected as relevant; all QUABs not copied from were annotated as irrelevant.
UIM_2:	Under this model, QUABs that users viewed were considered to be relevant; QUABs that remained unviewed were annotated as irrelevant.
UIM_3:	Under this model, QUABs that were either viewed or copied from were marked as relevant; all other QUABs were annotated as irrelevant.

Figure 4: User Interaction Models.

With FERRET, users are presented with as many as ten QUABs for every question they submit to the system. QUABs – whether they be generated automatically by FERRET's QUAB generation module, or selected from FERRET's knowledge base of over 10,000 manually-generated question/answer pairs – are presented in terms of their conceptual similarity to the original question. Conceptual similarity (as first described in (Harabagiu et al., 2005a)) is calculated using the version of the cosine similarity formula presented in Figure 5.

Conceptual Similarity weights content terms in Q_1 and Q_2 using $tfidf$ ($w_i = w(t_i) = (1 + \log(tf_i))\frac{\log N}{df_i}$), where N is the number of questions in the QUAB collection, while df_i is equal to the number of questions containing t_i and tf_i is the number of times t_i appears in Q_1 and Q_2. The questions Q_1 and Q_2 can be transformed into two vectors, $v_q = \langle w_{q_1}, w_{q_2}, ..., w_{q_m} \rangle$ and $v_u = \langle w_{u_1}, w_{u_2}, ..., w_{u_n} \rangle$; The similarity between Q_1 and Q_2 is measured as the cosine measure between their corresponding vectors:

$$\cos(v_q, v_u) = (\sum_i w_{q_i} w_{u_i})/((\sum_i w_{q_i}^2)^{\frac{1}{2}} \times (\sum_i w_{u_i}^2)^{\frac{1}{2}})$$

Figure 5: Conceptual Similarity.

In the three models from Figure 4, we allowed users to perform research as they normally would. Instead of requiring users to provide explicit forms of feedback, features were derived from the set of hyper-links that users selected and the text passages that users copied to the system clipboard.

Following (Kristjansson et al., 2004) we analyzed the performance of each of these three models using a new metric derived from the number of relevant QUABs that were predicted to be returned for each model. We calculated this metric – which we refer to as the Expected Number of Irrelevant QUABs – using the formula:

$$p_0(n) = \sum_{k=1}^{10} kp_0(k) \tag{1}$$

$$p_1(n) = (1 - p_0(0)) + \sum_{k=1}^{10} kp_1(k) \tag{2}$$

where $p_m(n)$ is equal to the probability of finding n irrelevant QUABs in a set of 10 suggestions returned to the user given m rounds of interaction. $p_0(n)$ (equation 1) is equal to the probability that all QUABs are relevant initially, while $p_1(n)$ (equation 2) is equal to the probability of finding an irrelevant QUAB after the set of QUABs has been interacted with by a user. For the purposes of this paper, we assumed that all of the QUABs initially returned by FERRET were relevant, and that $p_0(0) = 1.0$. This enabled us to calculate p_1(n) for each of the three models provided in Figure 4.

4.2 Relevance Estimation using Conditional Random Fields

Following work done by (Kristjansson et al., 2004), we used the feedback gathered in Section 4.1 to estimate the probability that a QUAB selected from FERRET'S PQN is, in fact, relevant to a user's original query. We assume that humans gauge the relevance of QUAB suggestions returned by the system by evaluating the informativeness of the QUAB with regards to the set of queries and suggestions that have occurred previously in the discourse. A QUAB, then, is deemed relevant when it conveys content that is sufficiently informative to the user, given what the user knows (i.e. the user's level of expertise) and what the user expects to receive as answers from the system.

Our approach treats a QUAB suggestion as a single node in a sequence of questions $\langle Q_{n-1}, Q_n, QUAB \rangle$ and classifies the QUAB as relevant or irrelevant based on features from the entire sequence.

We have performed relevance estimation using Conditional Random Fields (CRF). Given a random variable x (corresponding to data points $\{x_1, \ldots, x_n\}$) and another random variable y (corresponding to a set of labels $\{y_1, \ldots, y_n\}$), CRFs can be used to calculate the conditional probability $p(y|x)$. Given a sequence $\{x_1, \ldots, x_n\}$ and set of labels $\{y_1, \ldots, y_n\}$, $p(y|x)$ can be defined as:

$$p(y|x) = \frac{1}{z_0} \exp \left(\sum_{n=1}^{N} \sum_{k} \lambda_k f_k(y_{i-1}, y_i, x, n) \right) \quad (3)$$

where z_0 is a normalization factor and λ_k is a weight learned for each feature vector $f_k(y_{i-1}, y_i, x, n)$.

We trained our CRF model in the following way. If we assume that Λ is a set of feature weights $(\lambda_0, \ldots, \lambda_k)$, then we expect that we can use maximum likelihood to estimate values for Λ given a set of training data pairs (x, y).

Training is accomplished by maximizing the log-likelihood of each labeled data point as in the following equation:

$$w_\Lambda = \sum_{i=1}^{N} \log(p_\Lambda(x_i|y_i)) \quad (4)$$

Again, following (Kristjansson et al., 2004), we used the CRF Viterbi algorithm to find the most likely sequence of data points assigned to each label category using the formula:

$$y^* = \arg\max_y p_\Lambda(y|x) \quad (5)$$

Motivated by the types of discourse relations that appear to exist between states in an interactive Q/A dialogue, we introduced a large number of features to estimate relevance for each QUAB suggestion. The features we used are presented in Figure 6

(a) Rank of QUAB: the rank (1, ..., 10) of the QUAB in question.
(b) Similarity: similarity of QUAB, Q_n and QUAB, Q_{n-1}.
(c) Relation likelihood: equal to the likelihood of each predicate-argument structure included in QUAB given all QUABs contained in FERRET's QUAB; calculated for Arg-0, Arg-1, and ArgM-TMP for each predicate found in QUAB suggestions. (Predicate-argument relations were identifi ed using a semantic parser trained on PropBank (Palmer et al., 2005) annotations.)
(d) Conditional Expected Answer Type likelihood: equal to the joint probability $p(EAT_{QUAB}|EAT_{question})$ calculated from a corpus of dialogues collected from human users of FERRET.
(e) Terms in common: real-valued feature equal to the number of terms in common between the QUAB and both Q_n and Q_{n-1}.
(f) Named Entities in common: same as terms in common, but calculated for named entities detected by LCC's CIEROLITE named entity recognition system.

Figure 6: Relevance Features.

In the next section, we describe how we utilized the user interaction model described in Subsection 4.1 in conjunction with this subsection in order to improve the relevance of QUAB suggestions returned to users.

5 Experimental Results

In this section, we describe results from two experiments that were conducted using data collected from human interactions with FERRET.

In order to evaluate the effectiveness of our relevance classifier, we gathered a total of 1000 questions from human dialogues with FERRET. 500 of these came from interactions (41 dialogues) where the user was a self-described "expert" on the topic; another selection of 500 questions came from a total of 23 dialogues resulting from interactions with users who described themselves as "novice" or were otherwise unfamiliar with a topic. In order to validate the user's self-assessment, we selected 5 QUABs at random from the set of manually created QUABs assembled for each topic. Users were asked to provide written answers to those questions. Users that were judged to have correctly answered three out of five questions were considered "experts" for the purpose of our experiments. Table 2 presents the breakdown of questions across these two conditions.

User Type	Unique Topics	# Dialogues	Avg # of Qs/dialogue	Total Qs
Expert	12	41	12.20	500
Novice	8	23	21.74	500
Total	12	64	15.63	1000

Table 2: Question Breakdown.

Each of these experiments were run using a version of FERRET that returned the top 10 most similar QUABs from a database that combined manually-created QUABs with the automatically-generated QUABs created for the user's question. While a total of 10,000 QUABs were returned to users during these experiments, only 3,998 of these QUABs were unique (39.98%).

We conducted two kinds of experiments with users. In the first set of experiments, users were asked to mark all of the relevant QUABs that FERRET returned in response to questions submitted by users. After performing research on a particular scenario, expert and novice users were then supplied with as many as 65 questions (and associated QUABs) taken from previously-completed dialogues on the same scenario; users were then asked to select checkboxes associated with QUABs that were relevant. In addition, we also had 2 linguists (who were familiar with all of the research scenarios but did not research any of them) perform the same task for all of the collected questions and QUABs. Results from these three sets of annotations are found in Table 3.

User Type	Users	# Qs	# QUABs	# rel. QUABs	% relevant	ENIQ(P_1)
Expert	6	250	2500	699	27.96%	5.88
Novice	4	250	2500	953	38.12%	3.73
Linguists	2	500	5000	2240	44.80%	3.53

Table 3: User Comparison.

As expected, experts believed QUABs to be significantly ($p < 0.05$) less relevant than novices, who found approximately 38.12% of QUABs to be relevant to the original question submitted by a user. In contrast, the two linguists found 44.8% of the QUABs to be relevant. This number may be artificially high: since the linguists did not engage in actual Q/A dialogues for each of the scenarios they were annotating, they may not have been appropriately prepared to make a relevance assessment.

In the second set of experiments, we used the UIM in Figure 4 to train CRF-based relevance classifiers. We obtained training data for UIM_1 ("copy-and-paste"-based), UIM_2 ("click"-based), and UIM_3 ("hybrid") from 16 different dialogue histories collected from 8 different novice users. During these dialogues, users were asked to perform research as they normally would; no special instructions were given to users to provide additional relevance feedback to the system. After the dialogues were completed, QUABs that were copied from or clicked were annotated as "relevant" examples (according to each UIM); the remaining QUABs were annotated as "irrelevant". Once features (as described in Table 3) were extracted and the classifiers were trained, they were evaluated on a set of 1000 QUABs (500 "relevant", 500 "irrelevant") selected at random from the annotations performed in the first experiment. Table 4 presents results from these two classifiers.

UIM_1	P	R	F ($\beta = 1$)
Irrelevant	0.9523	0.9448	0.9485
Relevant	0.3137	0.3478	0.3299
UIM_2	P	R	F ($\beta = 1$)
Irrelevant	0.8520	0.8442	0.8788
Relevant	0.3214	0.4285	0.3673
UIM_3	P	R	F ($\beta = 1$)
Irrelevant	0.9384	0.9114	0.9247
Relevant	0.3751	0.3961	0.3853

Table 4: Experimental Results from 3 User Models.

Our results suggest that feedback gathered from a user's "normal" interactions with FERRET could be used to provide valuable input to a relevance classifier for QUABs When "copy-and-paste" events were used to train the classifier, the system detected instances of irrelevant QUABs with over 80% F. When the much more frequent "clicking" events were used to train the classifier, irrelevant QUABs were detected at over 90%F for both UIM_2 and UIM_3. In each of these three cases, however, detection of relevant QUABs lagged behind significantly: relevant QUABs were detected at 42% F in UIM_1 at nearly 33% F under UIM_2 and at 39% under UIM_3.

We feel that these results suggest that the detection of relevant QUABs (or the filtering of irrelevant QUABs) may be feasible, even without requiring users to provide additional forms of explicit feedback to the system. While we acknowledge that training models on these types of events may not always provide reliable sources of training data – especially as users copy or click on QUAB passages that may not be relevant to their interests in the research scenario, we believe the initial performance of these suggests that accurate forms of relevance feedback can be gathered without the use of mixed-initiative clarification dialogues.

6 Conclusions

In this paper, we have presented a methodology that combines feedback that was gathered from users in conjunction with a CRF-based classifier in order to enhance the quality of suggestions returned to users of interactive Q/A systems. We have shown that the irrelevant QUAB suggestions can be identified at over 90% when systems combine information from a user's interaction with semantic and pragmatic features derived from the structure and coherence of an interactive Q/A dialogue.

7 Acknowledgments

This material is based upon work funded in whole or in part by the U.S. Government and any opinions, findings, conclusions, or recommendations expressed in this material are those of the authors and do not necessarily reflect the views of the U.S. Government.

References

Sanda Harabagiu, Andrew Hickl, John Lehmann, and Dan Moldovan. 2005a. Experiments with Interactive Question-Answering. In *Proceedings of the 43rd Annual Meeting of the Association for Computational Linguistics (ACL'05).*

S. Harabagiu, D. Moldovan, C. Clark, M. Bowden, A. Hickl, and P. Wang. 2005b. Employing Two Question Answering Systems in TREC 2005. In *Proceedings of the Fourteenth Text REtrieval Conference.*

Sanda Harabagiu. 2004. Incremental Topic Representations. In *Proceedings of the 20th COLING Conference.*

Andrew Hickl, John Lehmann, John Williams, and Sanda Harabagiu. 2004. Experiments with Interactive Question-Answering in Complex Scenarios. In *Proceedings of the Workshop on the Pragmatics of Question Answering at HLT-NAACL 2004.*

T. Kristjansson, A. Culotta, P. Viola, and A. McCallum. 2004. Interactive information extraction with constrained conditional random fi elds. In *Proceedings of AAAI-2004.*

Chin-Yew Lin and Eduard Hovy. 2000. The Automated Acquisition of Topic Signatures for Text Summarization. In *Proceedings of the 18th COLING Conference.*

A. McCallum. 2003. Effi ciently inducing features of conditional random fi elds. In *Proceedings of the Nineteenth Conference on Uncertainty in Artificial Intelligence (UAI03).*

M. Palmer, D. Gildea, and P. Kingsbury. 2005. The Proposition Bank: An Annotated Corpus of Semantic Roles. In *Computational Linguistics*, 31(1):71–106.

Jean Scholtz and Emile Morse. 2003. Using consumer demands to bridge the gap between software engineering and usability engineering. In *Software Process: Improvement and Practice*, 8(2):89–98.

F. Sha and F. Pereira. 2003. *Shallow parsing with conditional random fields.* In *Proceedings of HLT-NAACL-2003.*

Sharon Small and Tomek Strzalkowski. 2004. HITIQA: Towards analytical question answering. In *Proceedings of Coling 2004.*

A Data Driven Approach to Relevancy Recognition for Contextual Question Answering

Fan Yang*
OGI School of Science & Engineering
Oregon Health & Science University
fly@cslu.ogi.edu

Junlan Feng and **Giuseppe Di Fabbrizio**
AT&T Labs - Research
180 Park Avenue, Florham Park, NJ, 07932 - USA
junlan@research.att.com, pino@research.att.com

Abstract

Contextual question answering (QA), in which users' information needs are satisfied through an interactive QA dialogue, has recently attracted more research attention. One challenge of engaging dialogue into QA systems is to determine whether a question is relevant to the previous interaction context. We refer to this task as relevancy recognition. In this paper we propose a data driven approach for the task of relevancy recognition and evaluate it on two data sets: the TREC data and the HandQA data. The results show that we achieve better performance than a previous rule-based algorithm. A detailed evaluation analysis is presented.

1 Introduction

Question Answering (QA) is an interactive human-machine process that aims to respond to users' natural language questions with exact answers rather than a list of documents. In the last few years, QA has attracted broader research attention from both the information retrieval (Voorhees, 2004) and the computational linguistic fields (http://www.clt.mq.edu.au/Events/Conferences/acl04qa/). Publicly accessible web-based QA systems, such as AskJeeves (http://www.ask.com/) and START (http://start.csail.mit.edu/), have scaled up this technology to open-domain solutions. More task-oriented QA systems are deployed as virtual customer care agents addressing questions about specific domains. For instance, the AT&T Ask Allie® agent (http://www.allie.att.com/) is able to answer questions about the AT&T plans and services; and the Ikea "Just Ask Anna!" agent (http://www.ikea.com/ms/en_US/) targets questions pertaining the company's catalog. Most of these QA systems, however, are limited to answer questions in isolation. The reality is that users often ask questions naturally as part of contextualized interaction. For instance, a question "How do I subscribe to the AT&T CallVantage® service?" is likely to be followed by other related questions like "How much will the basic plan cost?" and so on. Furthermore, many questions that users frequently want answers for cannot be satisfied with a simple answer. Some of them are too complicated, broad, narrow, or vague resulting that there isn't a simple good answer or there are many good answer candidates, which entails a clarification procedure to constrain or relax the search. In all these cases, a question answering system that is able to answer contextual questions is more favored.

Contextual question answering as a research challenge has been fostered by TREC (Text Retrieval Conference) since 2001. The TREC 2001 QA track made the first attempt to evaluate QA systems' ability of tracking context through a series of questions. The TREC 2004 re-introduced this task and organized all questions into 64 series, with each series focusing on a specific topic. The earlier questions in a series provide context for the on-going question. However, in reality, QA systems will not be

*The work was done when the first author was visiting AT&T Labs - Research.

Proceedings of the Interactive Question Answering Workshop at HLT-NAACL 2006, pages 33–40,
New York City, NY, USA. June 2006.

informed about the boundaries between series in advance.

One challenge of engaging dialogue into QA systems is to determine the boundaries between topics. For each question, the system would need to determine whether the question begins a new topic or it is a follow-up question related to the current existing topic. We refer to this procedure as *relevancy recognition*. If a question is recognized as a follow-up question, the next step is to make use of context information to interpret it and retrieve the answer. We refer to this procedure as *context information fusion*. Relevancy recognition is similar to text segmentation (Hearst, 1994), but relevancy recognition focuses on the current question with the previous text while text segmentation has the full text available and is allowed to look ahead.

De Boni and Manandhar (2005) developed a rule-based algorithm for relevancy recognition. Their rules were manually deduced by carefully analyzing the TREC 2001 QA data. For example, if a question has no verbs, it is a follow-up question. This rule-based algorithm achieves 81% in accuracy when recognizing the question relevance in the TREC 2001 QA data set. The disadvantage of this approach is that it involves a good deal of human effort to research on a specific data set and summarize the rules. For a new corpus from a different domain, it is very likely that one would have to go over the data set and modify the rules, which is time and human-effort consuming. An alternative is to pursue a data driven approach to automatically learn the rules from a data set. In this paper, we describe our experiments of using supervised learning classification techniques for the task of relevancy recognition. Experiments show that machine learning approach achieves better recognition accuracy and can also be easily applied to a new domain.

The organization of this paper is as follows. In Section 2, we summarize De Boni and Manandhar's rule-based algorithm. We present our learning approach in Section 3. We ran our experiments on two data sets, namely, the TREC QA data and the HandQA data, and give the results in Section 4. In section 5, we report our preliminary study on context information fusion. We conclude this paper in Section 6.

2 Rule-Based Approach

De Boni and Manandhar (2005) observed the following cues to recognize follow-up questions:

- *Pronouns and possessive adjectives*. For example, if a question has a pronoun that does not refer to an entity in the same sentence, this question could be a follow-up question.
- *Cue words*, such as "precisely" and "exactly".
- *Ellipsis*. For example, if a question is not syntactically complete, this question could be a follow-up question.
- *Semantic Similarity*. For example, if a question bears certain semantic similarity to previous questions, this question might be a follow-up question.

  De Boni and Manandhar (2005) proposed an algorithm of calculating the semantic similarity between the current question Q and a previous question Q'. Supposed Q consists of a list of words $(w_1, w_2, ..., w_n)$ and Q' consists of $(w'_1, w'_2, ..., w'_m)$:

  $$SentenceSimilarity(Q, Q') = \sum_{1 \le j \le n} \left(\max_{1 \le i \le m} WordSimilarity(w_j, w'_i) \right) \quad (1)$$

  The value of $WordSimilarity(w, w')$ is the similarity between two words, calculated from WordNet (Fellbaum, 1998). It returns a value between 0 (w and w' have no semantic relations) and 1 (w and w' are the same).

Motivated by these observations, De Boni and Manandhar (2005) proposed the rule-based algorithm for relevancy recognition given in Figure 1. This approach can be easily mapped into an handcrafted decision tree. According to the algorithm, a question follows the current existing topic if it (1) contains reference to other questions; or (2) contains context-related cue words; or (3) contains no verbs; or (4) bears certain semantic similarity to previous questions or answer. Evaluated on the TREC 2001 QA context track data, the recall of the algorithm is 90% for recognizing first questions and 78% for follow-up questions; the precision is 56% and 76% respectively. The overall accuracy is 81%.

Given the current question Q_i and a sequence of history questions Q_{i-n}, ..., Q_{i-1}:

1. *If Q_i has a pronoun or possessive adjective which has no references in the current question, Q_i is a follow-up question.*
2. *If Q_i has cue words such as "precisely" or "exactly", Q_i is a follow-up question.*
3. *If Q_i does not contain any verbs, Q_i is a follow-up question.*
4. *Otherwise, calculate the semantic similarity measure of Q_i as*

   $$SimilarityMeasure(Q_i) = \max_{1 \le j \le n} f(j) \cdot SentenceSimilarity(Q_i, Q_{i-j})$$

   Here f(j) is a decay function. If the similarity measure is higher than a certain threshold, Q_i is a follow-up question.
5. *Otherwise, if answer is available, calculate the semantic distance between Q_i and the immediately previous answer A_{i-1}: $SentenceSimilarity(Q_i, A_{i-1})$. If it is higher than a certain threshold, Q_i is a follow-up question that is related to the previous answer.*
6. *Otherwise, Q_i begins a new topic.*

Figure 1: Rule-based Algorithm

3 Data Driven Approach

3.1 Decision Tree Learning

As a move away from heuristic rules, in this paper, we make an attempt towards the task of relevancy recognition using machine learning techniques. We formulate it as a binary classification problem: a question either begins a new topic or follows the current existing topic. This classification task can be approached with a number of learning algorithms such as support vector machines, Adaboost and artificial neural networks. In this paper, we present our experiments using Decision Tree. A decision tree is a tree in which each internal node represents a choice between a number of alternatives, and each leaf node represents a decision. Learning a decision tree is fairly straightforward. It begins from the root node which consists of all the training data, growing the tree top-down by recursively splitting each node based on maximum information gain until certain criteria is met. Although the idea is simple, decision tree learning is often able to yield good results.

3.2 Feature Extraction

Inspired by De Boni and Manandhar's (2005) work, we selected two categories of features: syntactic features and semantic features. Syntactic features capture whether a question has certain syntactic components, such as verbs or pronouns. Semantic features characterize the semantic similarity between the current question and previous questions.

3.2.1 Syntactic Features

As the first step, we tagged each question with part-of-speech tags using GATE (Cunningham et al., 2002), a software tool set for text engineering. We then extracted the following binary syntactic features:

PRONOUN: whether the question has a pronoun or not. A more useful feature would be to label whether a pronoun refers to an entity in the previous questions or in the current question. However, the performances of currently available tools for anaphora resolution are quite limited for our task. The tools we tried, including GATE (Cunningham et al., 2002), LingPipe (`http://www.alias-i.com/lingpipe/`) and JavaRAP (Qiu et al., 2004), tend to use the nearest noun phrase as the referents for pronouns. While in the TREC questions, pronouns tend to refer to the topic words (focus). As a result, unsupervised anaphora resolution introduced more noise than useful information.

ProperNoun: whether the question has a proper noun or not.

NOUN: whether the question has a noun or not.

VERB: whether the question has a verb or not.

DefiniteNoun: if a question has a definite noun phrase that refers to an entity in previous questions, the question is very likely to be a follow-up question. However, considering the difficulty in automatically identifying definite noun phrases and their referents, we ended up not using this feature in our training because it in fact introduced misleading information.

3.3 Semantic Features

To compute the semantic similarity between two questions, we modified De Boni and Manandhar's formula with a further normalization by the length of the questions; see formula (2).

$$SentenceSimilarity(Q, Q') \quad (2)$$
$$= \frac{1}{n} \sum_{1 \le j \le n} (\max_{1 \le i \le m} WordSimilarity(w_j, w'_i))$$

This normalization has pros and cons. It removes the bias towards long sentences by eliminating the accumulating effect; but on the other hand, it might cause the system to miss a related question, for example, when two related sentences have only one key word in common.[1]

Formula (2) shows that sentence level similarity depends on word-word similarity. Researchers have proposed a variety of ways in measuring the semantic similarity or relatedness between two words (to be exact, word senses) based on WordNet. For example, the *Path (path) measure* is the inverse of the shortest path length between two word senses in WordNet; the *Wu and Palmer's (wup) measure* (Wu and Palmer, 1994) is to find the most specific concept that two word senses share as ancestor (least common subsumer), and then scale the path length of this concept to the root note (supposed that there is a virtual root note in WordNet) by the sum of the path lengths of the individual word sense to the root node; the *Lin's (lin) measure* (Lin, 1998) is based on information content, which is a corpus based measure of the specificity of a word; the *Vector (vector) measure* associates each word with a gloss vector and calculates the similarity of two words as the cosine between their gloss vectors (Patwardhan, 2003). It was unclear which measure(s) would contribute the best information to the task of relevancy recognition, so we just experimented on all four measures, path, wup, lin, and vector, in our decision tree training. We used Pedersen et al.'s (2004) tool *WordNet::Similarity* to compute these four measures. WordNet::Similarity implements nine different measures of word similarity. We here only used the four described above because they return a value between 0 and 1, which is suitable for using formula (2) to calculate sentence similarity, and we leave others as future work. Notice that the WordNet::Similarity implementation can only measure *path*, *wup*, and *lin* between two nouns or between two verbs, while it uses all the content words for the *vector* measure. We thus have the following semantic features:

path_noun: sentence similarity is based on the nouns[2] similarity using the *path* measure.

path_verb: sentence similarity is based on the non-trivial verbs similarity using the *path* measure. Trivial verbs include "does, been, has, have, had, was, were, am, will, do, did, would, might, could, is, are, can, should, shall, being".

wup_noun: sentence similarity is based on the nouns similarity using the *Wu and Palmer's* measure.

wup_verb: sentence similarity is based on the non-trivial verbs similarity using the *Wu and Palmer's* measure.

lin_noun: sentence similarity is based on the nouns similarity using the *Lin's* measure.

lin_verb: sentence similarity is based on the non-trivial verbs similarity using the *Lin's* measure.

vector: sentence similarity is based on all content words (nouns, verbs, and adjectives) similarity using the *vector* measure.

4 Results

We ran the experiments on two sets of data: the TREC QA data and the HandQA data.

4.1 Results on the TREC data

TREC has contextual questions in 2001 context track and 2004 (Voorhees, 2001; Voorhees, 2004). Questions about a specific topic are organized into a session. In reality, the boundaries between sessions are not given. The QA system would have to recognize the start of a new session as the first step of question answering. We used the TREC 2004 data as training and the TREC 2001 context track data as testing. The training data contain 286 factoid and list questions in 65 sessions[3]; the testing data contain 42 questions in 10 sessions. Averagely each session has about 4-5 questions. Figure 2 shows some example questions (the first three sessions) from the TREC 2001 context track data.

[1]Another idea is to feed the decision tree training both the normalized and non-normalized semantic similarity information and see what would come out. We tried it on the TREC data and found out that the normalized features actually have higher information gain (i.e. appear at the top levels of the learned tree.

[2]This is to filter out all other words but nouns from a sentence for measuring semantic similarity.

[3]In the TREC 2004 data, each session of questions is assigned a phrase as the topic, and thus the first question in a session might have pronouns referring to this topic phrase. In such cases, we manually replaced the pronouns by the topic phrase.

CTX1a	Which museum in Florence was damaged by a major bomb explosion in 1993?
CTX1b	On what day did this happen?
CTX1c	Which galleries were involved?
CTX1d	How many people were killed?
CTX1e	Where were these people located?
CTX1f	How much explosive was used?
CTX2a	Which industrial sector supplies the most jobs in Toulouse?
CTX2b	How many foreign companies were based there in 1994?
CTX2c	Name a company that flies there.
CTX3a	What grape variety is used in Chateau Petrus Bordeaus?
CTX3b	How much did the future cost for the 1989 Vintage?
CTX3c	Where did the winery's owner go to college?
CTX3d	What California winery does he own?

Figure 2: Example TREC questions

4.1.1 Confusion Matrix

Table 1 shows the confusion matrix of the decision tree learning results. On the testing data, the learned model performs with 90% in recall and 82% in precision for recognizing first questions; for recognizing follow-up questions, the recall is 94% and precision is 97%. In contrast, De Boni and Manandhar's rule-based algorithm has 90% in recall and 56% in precision for recognizing first questions; for follow-up questions, the recall is 78% and precision is 96%. The recall and precision of our learned model to recognize first questions and follow-up questions are all better than or at least the same as the rule-based algorithm. The accuracy of our learned model is 93%, about 12% absolute improvement from the rule-based algorithm, which is 81% in accuracy. Although the size of the data is too small to draw a more general conclusion, we do see that the data driven approach has better performance.

	Training Data			
	Predicted Class			
True Class	First	follow-up	Total	
First	63	2	65	
follow-up	1	220	221	
Total	64	222	286	

	Testing Data			
	Predicted Class			
True Class	First	follow-up	Total	Recall
First	9	1	10	90%
follow-up	2	30	32	94%
Total	11	31	42	
Precision	82%	97%		

Table 1: Confusion Matrix for TREC Data

4.1.2 Trained Tree

Figure 3 shows the first top two levels of the tree learned from the training data. Not surprisingly, *PRONOUN* turns out to be the most important feature which has the highest information gain. In the TREC data, when there is a pronoun in a question, the question is very likely to be a follow-up question. In fact, in the TREC 2004 data, the referent of pronouns very often is the topic phrase. The feature *path_noun*, on the second level of the trained tree, turns out to contribute most information in this recognition task among the four different semantic similarity measures. The similarity measures using *wup*, *wup_noun* and *wup_verb*, and the *vector* measure do not appear in any node of the trained tree.

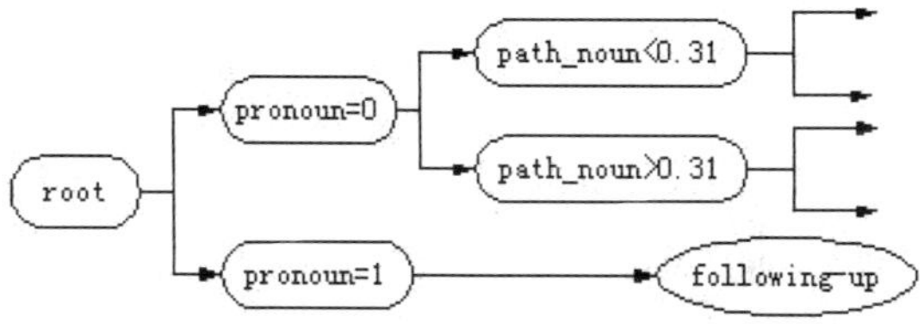

Figure 3: Trained Tree on TREC Data

The following are rules generated from the training data whose confidence is higher than 90%. Confidence is defined as out of the training records for which the left hand side of the rule is true, the percentage of records for which the right hand side is also true. This measures the accuracy of the rule.

- If *PRONOUN*=1 then follow-up question
- If *path_noun*≥0.31 then follow-up question
- If *lin_noun*≥0.43 then follow-up question
- If *path_noun*<0.15 and *PRONOUN*=0 then first question

De Boni and Manandhar's algorithm has this rule:"if a question has no verb, the question is follow-up question". However, we did not learn this rule from the data, nor the feature *VERB* appears in any node of the trained tree. One possible reason is that this rule has too little *support* in the training set (support is defined as the percentage of which the left hand side of the rule is true). Another possible reason is that this rule is not needed because the combination of other features is able to provide enough information for recognizing follow-up questions. In any case, the decision tree learns a (local) optimized combination of features which captures most cases, and avoids redundant rules.

4.1.3 Error Analysis

The trained decision tree has 3 errors in the testing data. Two of the errors are mis-recognition of follow-up questions to be first questions, and one is the vice versa.

The first error is failure to recognize the question "which galleries were involved?" (CTX1c) as a follow-up question (see Figure 2 for context). It is a syntactically complete sentence, and there is no pronoun or definite noun in the sentence. Semantic features are the most useful information to recognize it as a follow-up question. However, the semantic relatedness in WordNet between the words "gallery" in the current question and "museum" in the first question of this session (CTX1a in Figure 2) is not strong enough for the trained decision tree to relate the two questions together.

The second error is failure to recognize the question "Where did the winery's owner go to college?" (CTX3c) as a follow-up question. Similarly, part of the reason for this failure is due to the insufficient semantic relatedness between the words "winery" and "grape" (in CTX3a) to connect the questions together. However, this question has a definite noun phrase "the winery" which refers to "Chateau Petrus Bordeaux" in the first question in this session. We did not make use of the feature *DefiniteNoun* in our training, because it is not easy to automatically identify the referents of a definite noun phrase, or even whether it has a referent or not. A lot of definite noun phrases, such as "the sun", "the trees in China", "the first movie", and "the space shuttles", do not refer to any entity in the text. This does not mean that the feature *DefiniteNoun* is not important, but instead that we just leave it as our future work to better incorporate this feature.

The third error, is failure to recognize the question "What does transgenic mean?" as the first question that opens a session. This error is due to the overfitting of decision tree training.

4.1.4 Boosting

We tried another machine learning approach, Adaboost (Schapire and Singer, 2000), which is resistant (but not always) to over-fitting. It calls a given weak learning algorithm repeatedly in a series of rounds $t = 1, ..., T$. Each time the weak learning algorithm generates a rough "rule of thumb", and after many rounds Adaboost combines these weak rules into a single prediction rule that, hopefully, will be more accurate than any one of the weak rules. Figure 2 shows the confusion matrix of Adaboost learning results. It shows that Adaboost is able to correctly recognize "What does transgenic mean?" as beginning a new topic. However, Adaboost has more errors in recognizing follow-up questions, which results in an overall accuracy of 88%, slightly lower than decision tree learning.

	Training Data			
	Predicted Class			
True Class	First	follow-up	Total	
First	64	1	65	
follow-up	1	220	221	
Total	65	221	286	

	Testing Data			
	Predicted Class			
True Class	First	follow-up	Total	Recall
First	10	0	10	100%
follow-up	5	27	32	84%
Total	15	27	42	
Precision	67%	100%		

Table 2: Confusion Matrix Using Adaboosting

4.2 Results on the HandQA data

We also conducted an experiment using real-world customer-care related questions. We selected our test data from the chat logs of a deployed online QA system. We refer to this system as HandQA. HandQA is built using a telecommunication ontology database and 1600 pre-determined FAQ-answer pairs. For every submitted customer question, HandQA chooses one of these 1600 answers as the response. Each chat session contains about 3 questions. We assume the questions in a session are context-related.

The HandQA data are different from the TREC data in two ways. First, HandQA questions are real typed questions from motivated users. The HandQA data contain some noisy information, such as typos and bad grammars. Some users even treated this system as a search engine and simply typed in the keywords. Second, questions in a chat session basically asked for the same information. Very often, when the system failed to get the correct answer to the user's question, the user would repeat or rephrase the same question, until they gave up or the system luckily found the answer. As an example, Figure 4 shows two chat sessions. Again, we did not use the system's answer in our relevancy recognition.

How to make number non published? Non published numbers How to make number non listed?
Is my number switched to Call Vantage yet? When will my number be switched? When is number transferred?

Figure 4: Example questions in HandQA

A subset of the HandQA data, 5908 questions in 2184 sessions are used for training and testing the decision tree. The data were randomly divided into two sets: 90% for training and 10% for testing.

4.2.1 Confusion Matrix

Table 3 shows the confusion matrix of the decision tree learning results. For recognizing first questions, the learned model has 73% in recall and 62% in precision; for recognizing follow-up questions, the recall is 75% and precision is 84%. The accuracy is 74%. A base line model is to have all questions except the first one as following up questions, which results in the accuracy of 64% (380/590). Thus the learned decision tree yields an absolute improvement of 10%. However, the results on this data set are not as good as those on the TREC data.

	Training Data Predicted Class			
True Class	First	follow-up	Total	
First	1483	490	1973	
follow-up	699	2646	3345	
Total	2182	3136	5318	
	Testing Data Predicted Class			
True Class	First	follow-up	Total	Recall
First	153	58	211	73%
follow-up	93	286	379	75%
Total	246	344	590	
Precision	62%	84%		

Table 3: Confusion Matrix for HandQA Data

4.2.2 Trained Tree

Table 5 shows the top two levels of the tree learned from the training data, both of which are on the semantic measure *path*. This again confirms that *path* best fits the task of relevancy recognition among the four semantic measures.

No syntactical features appear in any node of the learned tree. This is not surprising because syntactic information is noisy in this data set. Typos, bad grammars, and mis-capitalization affect automatic POS tagging. Keywords input also results in incomplete sentences, which makes it unreliable to recognize follow-up questions based on whether a question is a complete sentence or not. Furthermore, because questions in a session rarely refer to each other, but just repeat or rephrase each other, the feature *PRONOUN* does not help either. All these make syntactic features not useful. Semantic features turn out to be more important for this data set.

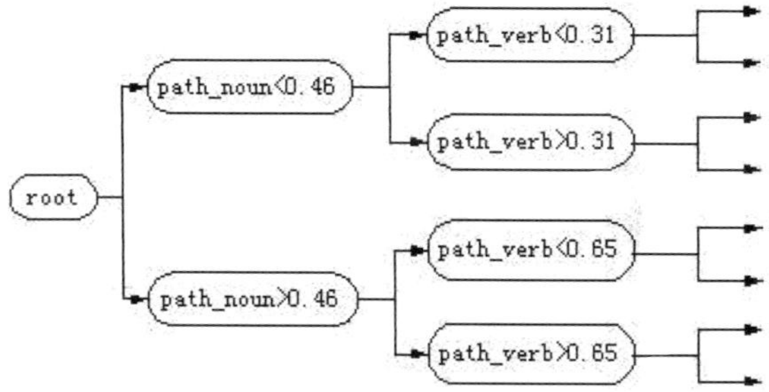

Figure 5: Trained Tree on HandQA Data

4.2.3 Error Analysis

There are two reasons for the decreased performance in this data set. The first reason, as we analyzed above, is that syntactical features do not contribute to the recognition task. The second reason is that consecutive chat sessions might ask for the same information. In the handQA data set, questions are basically all about telecommunication service, and questions in two consecutive chat sessions, although by different users, could be on very similar topics or even have same words. Thus, questions, although in two separate chat sessions, could have high semantic similarity measure. This would introduce confusing information to the decision tree learning.

5 Making Use of Context Information

Relevancy recognition is the first step of contextual question answering. If a question is recognized as following the current existing topic, the next step is to make use of the context information to interpret it and retrieve the answers. To explore how context information helps answer retrieval, we conducted preliminary experiments with the TREC 2004 QA data. We indexed the TREC documents using the Lucene search engine (Hatcher and Gospodnetic, 2004) for document retrieval. The Lucene search engine takes as input a query (a list of keywords), and returns a ranked list of relevant documents, of which the first 50 were taken and analyzed in our experiments. We tried different strategies for query formulation. Simply using the questions as the query, only 20% of the follow-up questions find their answers in the first 50 returned documents. This percentage went up to 85% when we used the topic words, provided in TREC data for each section, as the query. Because topic words are usually not available in real world applications, to be more practical, we tried using the noun phrases in the first question as the query. In this case, 81% of the questions are able to find the answers in the returned documents. When we combined the (follow-up) question with the noun phrases in the first question as the query, the retrieved rate increases to 84%. Typically, document retrieval is a crucial step for QA systems. These results suggest that context information fusion has a big potential to improve the performance of answer retrieval. However, we leave the topic of how to fuse context information into the follow-up questions as future work.

6 Conclusion

In this paper, we present a data driven approach, decision tree learning, for the task of relevancy recognition in contextual question answering. Experiments show that this approach achieves 93% accuracy on the TREC data, about 12% improvement from the rule-based algorithm reported by De Boni and Mananhar (2005). Moreover, this data driven approach requires much less human effort on investigating a specific data set and less human expertise to summarize rules from the observation. All the features we used in the training can be automatically extracted. This makes it straightforward to train a model in a new domain, such as the HandQA. Furthermore, decision tree learning is a white-box model and the trained tree is human interpretable. It shows that the *path* measure has the best information gain among the other semantic similarity measures. We also report our preliminary experiment results on context information fusion for question answering.

7 Acknowledgement

The authors thank Srinivas Bangalore and Mazin E. Gilbert for helpful discussion.

References

Hamish Cunningham, Diana Maynard, Kalina Bontcheva, and Valentin Tablan. 2002. GATE: A framework and graphical development environment for robust nlp tools and applications. In *Proceedings of the 40th ACL.*

Marco De Boni and Suresh Manandhar. 2005. Implementing clarification dialogues in open domain question answering. *Natural Language Engineering.* Accepted.

Christiane Fellbaum. 1998. *WordNet:An Electronic Lexical Database.* MIT Press, Cambridge, MA.

Erik Hatcher and Otis Gospodnetic. 2004. *Lucene in Action.* Manning.

Marti A. Hearst. 1994. Multi-paragraph segmentation of expository text. In *Proceedings of 32nd ACL*, pages 9–16.

Dekang Lin. 1998. An information-theoretic definition of similarity. In *Proceedings of the International Conference on Machine Learning.*

Siddharth Patwardhan. 2003. Incorporating dictionary and corpus information into a context vector measure of semantic relatedness. master's thesis, University of Minnesota, Duluth.

Ted Pederson, Siddharth Patwardhan, and Jason Michelizzi. 2004. WordNet::Similarity - measuring the relatedness of concepts. In *Proceedings of the 9th AAAI.* Intelligent Systems Demonstration.

Long Qiu, Min-Yen Kan, and Tat-Seng Chua. 2004. A public reference implementation of the rap anaphora resolution algorithm. In *Proceedings of LREC*, pages 291–294.

Robert E. Schapire and Yoram Singer. 2000. BoosTexter: A boosting-based system for text categorization. *Machine Learning*, 39:135–168.

Ellen M. Voorhees. 2001. Overview of the TREC 2001 question answering track. In *Proceedings of TREC-10.*

Ellen M. Voorhees. 2004. Overview of the TREC 2004 question answering track. In *Proceedings of TREC-13.*

Zhibiao Wu and Martha Palmer. 1994. Verb semantics and lexical selection. In *Proceedings of 32nd ACL*, pages 133–138.

Answering questions of Information Access Dialogue (IAD) task using ellipsis handling of follow-up questions

Junichi Fukumoto
Department of Media Technology
Ritsumeikan University
1-1-1 Nojihigashi, Kusatsu, Shiga 525-8577 Japan
fukumoto@media.ritsumei.ac.jp

Abstract

In this paper, we propose ellipsis handling method for follow-up questions in Information Access Dialogue (IAD) task of NTCIR QAC3. In this method, our system classifies ellipsis patterns of question sentences into three types and recognizes elliptical elements using ellipsis handling algorithm for each type. In the evaluation using Formal Run and Reference Run data, there were several cases which our algorithm could not handle ellipsis correctly. According to the analysis of evaluation results, the main reason of low performance was lack of word information for recognition of referential elements. If our system can recognize word meanings correctly, some errors will not occur and ellipsis handling works well.

1 Introduction

In question answering task QAC of NTCIR (Kato et al., 2005)(Kato et al., 2004), interactive use of question answering is proposed as one of evaluation task called Information Access Dialogue (IAD) task, which was called *subtask3* in QAC1,2. In IAD task, a set of question consists of one first question and several follow-up questions. These series of questions and answers comprise an information access dialogue. In QAC1, there was only one follow-up question in a series of questions, but in QAC2 and 3 there were several follow-up questions.

All follow-up questions have anaphoric expressions including zero anaphora which is frequently occurs in Japanese. There were several approaches to answer follow-up questions. One approach was to extract answers of follow-up questions from documents which were retrieved using clue words of the first question (Sasaki et al., 2002). In the other approach, they added clue words extracted from the previous questions to clue words of follow-up question for document retrieval (Murata et al., 2002). However, when topic was changed in a series of questions, these approaches did not work well because clue words of the previous questions were not always effective to extract answer of the current question.

Our approach is to handle ellipses of follow-up questions and apply the processed questions to ordinary question answering system which extracts answers of a question (Fukumoto et al., 2002)(Fukumoto et al., 2004)(Matsuda and Fukumoto, 2005). For QAC3, we have improved our previous approach to handle follow-up questions, that is, we have expanded ellipsis handling rules more precisely. Based on the analysis of evaluation results of QAC2, we have classified ellipsis pattern of question sentences into three types. The first type is ellipsis using pronoun. This is the case that a word used in previous questions is replaced with pronoun. The second type is ellipsis of word in verb's obligatory case elements in the follow-up question. Some obligatory case elements of a verb of a follow-up question will be omitted and such elements also used in the previous question. The last type is ellipsis of a modifier or modificand in a follow-up question. Such an ele-

Proceedings of the Interactive Question Answering Workshop at HLT-NAACL 2006, pages 41–48,
New York City, NY, USA. June 2006.

ment appears in the previous question and has modification relationship with some word in the follow-up question sentence. In order to handle the above three ellipsis types, we utilized case information of main verb of a question and co-occurrence of nouns to recognize which case information is omitted. We used co-occurrence dictionary which was developed by Japan Electric Dictionary Research Inc. (EDR) (EDR,).

As for core QA system which is our main question answering system, we have integrated previous systems modules which are developed for QAC2. One module is to handle numeric type questions. It analyzes co-occurrence data of unit expression and their object names and detects an appropriate numeric type. Another module uses detailed classification of Named Entity for non numerical type questions such as person name, organization name and so on to extract an answer element of a given question.

In the following sections, we will show the details of analysis of elliptical question sentences and our new method of ellipsis handling. We will also discuss our system evaluation on ellipsis handling.

2 Ellipsis handling

In this section, we explain what kinds of ellipsis patterns exist in the follow-up questions of a series of questions and how to resolve each ellipsis to apply them to core QA system.

2.1 Ellipsis in questions

We have analyzed 319 questions (46sets) which were used in subtask3 of QAC1 and QAC2 and then, classified ellipsis patterns into 3 types as follows:

Replacing with pronoun

In this pattern, pronoun is used in a follow-up question and this pronoun refers an element or answer of the previous question.

Ex1-1 アメリカの大統領は誰ですか。
(Who is the president of America?)

Ex1-2 そこが独立したのはいつですか。
(When did it become independent?)

In the above example, pronoun "そこ (it)" of question **Ex1-2** refers a word "アメリカ (America)" of question **Ex1-1**. The question **Ex1-2** should be " アメリカが独立したのはいつですか。(When does America become independent?)" in a completed form.

Ex2-1 アメリカの大統領は誰ですか。
(Who is the president of America?)

Ex2-2 彼の出身地はどこですか。
(Where is his birth place?)

In the above example, pronoun "彼 (his)" of question **Ex2-2** refers an answer word "ブッシュ (J. Bush)" of question **Ex2-1**. The question **Ex2-2** should be "ブッシュの出身地はどこですか。(Where is J. Bush's birth place?)" in a completed form.

Ellipsis of an obligatory case element of verb

In this pattern, an obligatory case element verb in follow-up question is omitted, and the omitted element refers an element or answer of the previous question. An example of this pattern is as follows:

Ex3-1 アメリカの大統領は誰ですか。
(Who is the president of America?)

Ex3-2 いつ就任しましたか。
(When did ϕ inaugurate?)

In the above example, the verb "就任する (inaugurate)" has two obligatory case frames "agent" and "goal", and the elements of each case frame are omitted. The element of "agent" is the answer of **Ex3-1**, and the element of "goal" is "大統領 (the President)" of **Ex3-1**. Therefore, **Ex3-2** should be "(the answer of **Ex3-1**) はいつ大統領に就任しましたか。(When did (the answer of **Ex3-1**) inaugurated as the President?)".

Ellipsis of a modifier or modificand

This pattern is the case of ellipsis of modifier. When there is modification relation between two words of a question, either of them (modifying element or the modified element) modifies an element of the next question but is omitted. We call the modifying element modifier and we call the modified element modificand. The following example shows ellipsis of modifier.

Ex4-1 アメリカの大統領は誰ですか。
(Who is the president of America?)

Ex4-2 国務長官は誰ですか。
(Who is a minister of state?)

In the above example, the word "アメリカ (America)" is modifier of "大統領 (the president)" in the question **Ex4-1**. Then, the word "アメリカ (America)" also modifies "国務長官 (a minister of state)" of **Ex4-2** and is also omitted. The question **Ex4-2** should be "アメリカの国務長官は誰ですか。(Who is a minister of state of America?)".

The following example shows ellipsis of modificand.

Ex5-1 アメリカの大統領は誰ですか。
(Who is the president of America?)

Ex5-2 フランスは誰ですか。
(Who is ϕ of France?)

In this example, the word "大統領 (the president)" is modificand of the word "アメリカ (America)" in the question **Ex5-1**. In the question **Ex5-2**, the word "フランス (France)" should modifies the word "大統領 (the president)" which is omitted in the question **Ex5-2**. Then the question **Ex5-2** should be "フランスの大統領は誰ですか。(Who is the president of France?)".

2.2 How to resolve ellipsis

2.2.1 Overview of the method

We will show ellipsis resolution method of these three patterns. For the first pattern, we replace the pronoun with a word which referred by it. For the second pattern, we try to fill up obligatory case frames of the verb. For the third pattern, we take a word from the previous question based on co-occurrence frequency. We assumed that the antecedent of an elliptical question exists in a question which appears just before, so the "previous question" indicates immediately previous question in our method. We show the process as follows:

Step1 Estimate the pattern of ellipsis:

When a follow-up question has pronoun, this is the case of the first pattern. When a follow-up question has some verb which has an omitted case element, this is the case of the second pattern. When a follow-up question has no pronoun and such a verb, this is the case of the third pattern.

Step2 Estimate kinds of the omitted word:

Step2a When the ellipsis pattern is the first pattern:

Estimate the kind of word which the pronoun refers. When the pronoun directly indicates kinds of word (ex: 彼: he), depend on it. If the pronoun does not directly indicate kinds of word (ex: その:its +noun), use the kind of the word which exists just behind the pronoun.

Step2b When the ellipsis pattern is the second pattern:

Estimate obligatory case frame of the verb of the follow-up question. Then, estimate omitted element of the case frame and the type of the element.

Step2c When the ellipsis pattern is the third pattern:

Get a noun X which appears with Japanese particle "は (ha)"[1] in the follow-up question. When compound noun appears with "は (ha)", the last word is assumed to be X. Then, collect words which are modifier or modificand of X from corpus. If the same word as collected words is in the previous question, take over the word and skip step3. Otherwise, estimate the kind of word which is suitable to modifier (or modificand) of X. Estimate the kind of collected modifiers and modificands, and adopt one which has the highest frequency.

Step3 Decide the succeeded word of the previous question:

Estimate type of answer of previous question [2] and kind of each word used in previous question from rear to front. When a word has a kind fit for the estimate in step2, take the word to follow-up question.

2.2.2 EDR thesauruses dictionary

We have used thesauruses of EDR dictionary to estimate the kind of words, obligatory case frame of verbs, omitted element of case frame, and to collect modifier and modificand of a word. Details are as follows:

Estimation of word type

We used EDR Japanese Word Dictionary and EDR Concept Dictionary. Japanese Word Dictionary records Japanese words and its detailed concept as Concept Code, and Concept Dictionary records each Concept Code and its upper concept. We check a target word using Japanese Word Dictionary and

[1]This particle is used as topic marker in Japanese.

[2]Use core QA's module

get its detailed concept code. Then, we generalize type of the word using concept code of Concept Dictionary.

For example, concept code of a word "会社 (company)" is *3ce735* which means "a group of people combined together for business or trade". We will check its upper concept using Concept Dictionary, for example, upper concept of *3ce735* is *4449f5*, upper concept of *4449f5* is *30f74c*, and so on. Finally, we can get word type of *3ce735* as *3aa912* which means "agent (self-functioning entity)". Therefore, we can estimate that type of word "会社 (company)" is an agent.

Estimation of obligatory case frame of verb and omitted element

We will use EDR Japanese Cooccurrence Dictionary for estimation of omitted case element. Japanese Cooccurrence Dictionary contains information of verb case frame and concept code with Japanese particle for each case. We will check obligatory case frame and omitted element. Firstly, we check a verb with Japanese Cooccurrence Dictionary and get its case frame, concept code and particle information. Then we can recognize omitted case element by particle information and estimate word type of omitted element.

For example, according to the Japanese Cooccurrence Dictionary, a verb "就任する (inaugurate)" has two case frames, agent (*30f6b0*) and goal (*3f98cb* or *3aa938*), and agent is used with particle "が (ga)", goal is used with particle "に (ni)". If question doesn't have any "が (ga)" or "に (ni)" (ex: "いつ就任しましたか。(When did ϕ inaugurate?)"), we estimate that agent and goal are omitted. Then, we estimate kind of the omitted element same as "Estimation of kind of words".

Collection of modifier and modificand

Japanese Cooccurrence Dictionary contains Japanese co-occurrence data of various modifications. We will use the co-occurrence data to collect modifier or modificand of word X. Details as follows:

1. Search "X の (no) noun (noun of X)" and "noun の (no) X (X of noun)" pattern from Japanese Cooccurrence Dictionary
2. When Y appears in the "Y の (no) X (X of Y)" pattern, we can estimate Y as modifier of X.
3. When Y appears in the "X の (no) Y (Y of X)" pattern, we can estimate Y as modificand of X.

2.2.3 Examples of ellipsis handling

We will show above examples of ellipsis handling in the following.

Example of ellipsis handling of first pattern[3]

Ex1-1	アメリカの大統領は誰ですか。 (Who is the president of America?)
Ex1-2	そこが独立したのはいつですか。 (When did it become independent?)
Ex1-2'	アメリカが独立したのはいつですか。 (When did America become independent?)

In the above example, **Ex1-2** has a pronoun "そこ (it)", so we classified ellipsis pattern of **Ex1-2** into the first pattern. Pronoun "そこ (it)" refers organization or location by information of pronoun. The word "アメリカ (America)" has information of location but the word "大統領 (the president)" are not organization or location. Then we can estimate that pronoun "そこ (it)" of **Ex1-2** refers the word "アメリカ (America)" of **Ex1-1**. Question **Ex1-2** should be "アメリカの大統領は誰ですか。(Who is the president of America?)" .

Example of ellipsis handling of second pattern

Ex3-1	アメリカの大統領は誰ですか。 (Who is the president of America?)
Ex3-2	いつ就任しましたか。 (When did he inaugurated?)
Ex3-2'	(answer of **Ex3-1**) はいつ大統領に就任しましたか。 (When did (answer of **Ex3-1**) inaugurated?)

In the above example, **Ex3-2** has a verb "就任する (inaugurate)", so we classified ellipsis pattern of **Ex3-2** into the second pattern. The word "就任する (inaugurate)" has two obligatory case: agent (human) and goal (managerial position). **Ex3-2** doesn't have word which is suitable for obligatory cases of "就任する (inaugurate)". Therefore we estimate that the agent and the goal are omitted. Then, we estimate answer type of **Ex3-1** and kind of each word of **Ex3-1**. The answer type of **Ex3-1** is human, so it

[3]**Exm-n'** indicates complemented question of **Exm-n**

is suitable for the agent. The kind of "大統領 (the president)" is managerial position, so it is suitable for the goal. Finally, we take the answer of **Ex3-1** and "大統領 (the president)" to **Ex3-2** and **Ex3-2** becomes "(answer of **Ex3-1**) はいつ大統領に就任しましたか。(When did (answer of **Ex3-1**) inaugurated?)" .

Example of ellipsis handling of third pattern

Ex4-1 アメリカの大統領は誰ですか。
(Who is the president of America?)
Ex4-2 国務長官は誰ですか。
(Who is a minister of state?)
Ex4-2' アメリカの国務長官は誰ですか。
(Who is a minister of state of America?)

In the above example, **Ex4-2** doesn't have any pronoun and verb, so we classified ellipsis pattern of **Ex4-2** into the third pattern. Then we search "noun の国務長官 (a minister of noun)" and "国務長官の noun (noun of a minister)" pattern from the Japanese Cooccurrence Dictionary. In the Japanese Cooccurrence Dictionary, we can find "アメリカの国務長官 (a minister of America)" pattern. "アメリカ (America)" is used in **Ex4-1**, so we take over "アメリカ (America)" to **Ex4-2** and **Ex4-2** becomes "アメリカの国務長官は誰ですか。 (Who is a minister of state of America?)".

3 Evaluation

3.1 Evaluation method

We have evaluated our QA system only on ellipses handling. The following example shows question sets of the Formal Run and Reference Run. In **Qm-n**, m and n indicates series ID and its question number which we gave and **Rm-n** indicates a question which correspond to **Qm-n**.

Questions of Formal Run

Q1-1 富士山レーダーはいつ設置されましたか。
(When was Mt.Fuji radar installed?)
(QAC3-30038-01)
Q1-2 どういう目的で設置されましたか。
(What kind of purpose was it installed by?)
(QAC3-30038-02)
Q1-3 富士山の何処にありましたか。
(Which area of Mt.Fuji was it installed?)
(QAC3-30038-03)
Q1-4 どのような表彰を受けましたか。
(What kind of award did it get?)
(QAC3-30038-04)

Questions of Reference Run

R1-1 富士山レーダーはいつ設置されましたか。
(When was Mt.Fuji radar installed?)
(QAC3-31267-01)
R1-2 富士山レーダーはどういう目的で設置されましたか。(What kind of purpose was Mt.Fuji radar installed by?)
(QAC3-31268-01)
R1-3 富士山レーダーは富士山の何処にありましたか。(Which area of Mt.Fuji was Mt. Fuji radar installed?)
(QAC3-31269-01)
R1-4 富士山レーダーはどのような表彰を受けましたか。(What kind of award did Mt. Fuji radar get?)
(QAC3-31270-01)

In IAD task, one series of questions consists of the first question and several follow-up questions which contain ellipsis. In our current implementation, we assumed that antecedent of an elliptical question exists in its just before question. For example, the antecedent of **Q1-2** is "富士山レーダー (Mt.Fuji radar)" of **Q1-1**. The antecedent of **Q1-4** is "富士山レーダー (Mt.Fuji radar)" of **Q1-1** actually, however, if **Q1-3** is completed correctly (as **R1-3**), "富士山レーダー (Mt.Fuji radar)" exists in **Q1-3**. Therefore, we prepared evaluation data from QAC test set, 310 pairs of questions. One pair consists of a question of Reference Run and a question of Formal Run. For example, **R1-1** and **Q1-2** is one pair of the evaluation data, **R1-3** and **Q1-4** is other one. We have evaluated our method using this data. Correctness has been judged by human. When the system must take an answer of previous question, we have used

"<ANS>" which indicates the answer of previous question. [4]

3.2 Results

Our system could complete 52 of 310 questions correctly as results. 28 among 52 success cases are done by ellipsis handling method proposed in the previous QAC evaluation. Our previous approach is based on topic presentation in question sentences. If there is an ellipsis in a question, we will use information of topic information in the previous question. Topic presentation is detected by Japanese particle "は (ha)". The other cases of 24 were succeeded by the approach described above. We will show the details as follows:

- Replacing with pronoun:

  System classified 88 of 310 questions in this pattern. The all of 88 classifications were correct. 12 of 88 questions were completed correctly.

- Ellipsis of an obligatory case element of verb:

  System classified 158 of 310 questions as this pattern. 105 of 158 classifications were correct. 8 of 105 questions were completed correctly.

- Ellipsis of a modifier or modificand:

  System classified 64 of 310 questions as this pattern. 44 of 64 classifications were correct. 4 of 44 questions were completed correctly.

Major failure cases and their numbers which are indicated with dots are as follows:

Failure of classification of ellipsis pattern

- System uses wrong verbs...29
- All obligatory cases of verb is filled and other element is omitted...22
- Failure of morphological analysis...8
- An adjective phrase is omitted...1

[4]In the Formal Run, we have replace "<ANS>" with the 1st answer of core QA. In the evaluation, considering core QA's failure, we have left "<ANS>" and considered as correct.

Failure of estimation of omitted element of follow-up question

- Verb isn't recorded in Japanese Cooccurrence Dictionary...35
- Shortage of rules for pronoun...17
- System fills up to case already filled up...15
- Any modifier or modificand doesn't exist in Japanese Cooccurrence Dictionary...10
- Case frame element is omitted but system fails to find it...7
- Verb is passive voice...6
- System fails to select the element of modification relation...6
- Question doesn't have element of case frame and it is unnecessary...2

Failure of decision of which word should be taken

- System fails to estimate word type of answer in the previous question...79
- System fails to decide to scope of target word...21
- A modifier or modificand which has lower cooccurrence frequency should be taken...7
- System takes inappropriate word from an interrogative phrase...6
- Answer type of the previous question has same kind with a word should be taken...3

4 Discussion

Our system could work well for some elliptical questions as described in the previous section. We will show some examples and detail of major failure analysis results in the following.

1. Verb case elements:

   There was a Japanese delexical verb[5] "いる" in a follow-up question, then our system could not

[5]Delexical verb is a functional verb which has specific meaning in it.

fill up its obligatory cases because every obligatory cases of this verb had already filled up. It is necessary to handle these delexical verbs such as "いる", "なる", "いう" and so on as stop words.

Otherwise, there were several questions in which all obligatory cases of verb has already filled up. In this case, it is necessary to apply the other approach. In the example "オープン初日のフィルムカット式に出席した俳優は誰でしたか。(What is the actor's name who attended opening event in the first day?)", some additional information for "opening event" is omitted. Moreover, there were some verbs which had no case information in EDR dictionary. It would be helpful to check co-occurrence with this word in the previous question.

2. Morphological analysis failure:

   The expression "そこで (sokode)" in question sentence was recognized as one conjunction "そこで (then)" although it should be analyzed in "そこ (soko: there)" + "で (de: at)". If morphological analyzer works well, our algorithm could handle ellipsis correctly.

3. Lack of rules for pronoun:

   In the expression "この宇宙ステーション (this space station)" of question sentence, ellipsis handling rule for pronoun "この (this)" was not implemented, then our method could not handle this case. It is necessary to expand our algorithm for this case.

4. case information handling error:

   q1 阿川佐和子がキャスターをしていたのはどこのテレビ局ですか。(Which TV station is Ms. Sawako Agawa working as TV caster?) (QAC3-31206-01)

   q2 初めて書いた長編小説は何ですか。(What is the title of long novel which ϕ firstly wrote?) (QAC3-30029-05)

   In the above example (q1 is the first question and q2 is follow-up question), system checks obligatory case elements of verb "書く (write)" of question q1. The verb "書く" has three obligatory cases: agent, object and goal according to EDR dictionary. System estimated that every obligatory case element were omitted, and checks "阿川佐和子 (Ms. Sawako Agawa)", "キャスター (TV caster)", "キャスター (TV caster)" respectively. However, object case of verb "書く" was "長編小説 (long novel)" of question q2 actually. In this question, this element was modified by verb "書く (write)", then system failed to estimate that the object was already filled. So, our algorithm tried to fill this object case up as "キャスター (TV caster)". It is necessary to improve patterns of estimation of omitted case element.

5. lack of co-occurrence information:

   q3 日光東照宮の例大祭は毎年いつ行われるのですか。(When is Reitaisai of Nikko Toshogu held in every year?) (QAC3-31235-01)

   q4 ハイライトは何ですか。(What is the highlight?)(QAC3-30033-06)

   q4' 日光東照宮のハイライトは何ですか。(What is the highlight of Nikko Toshogu?)

   In the above example, q3 is the first question and q4 is the follow-up question. The question q4 is replaced with q4' using ellipsis handling. In this case, system took wrong modifier "日光東照宮 (Nikko Toshogu)" for "ハイライト (highlight)". It is caused by lack of co-occurrence information in EDR Japanese Cooccurrence Dictionary because these words are proper nouns which are not frequently used. In order to handle such cases, it is necessary to use co-occurrence information using large corpus.

6. Passive verb expression:

   In our current implementation, our system has no rule to handle passive verb. In case of passive voice, it is necessary to check other case element for ellipsis handling.

7. Multiple candidates:

q5 コリン・パウエルは誰に国務長官に指名されたのですか。(Who appointed Mr. Collin Powell as a minister of state?) (QAC3-31087-01)

q6 彼の政治的な立場はどのようなものですか。(What is his political situation?) (QAC3-30013-03)

q6' <ANS> の政治的な立場はどのようなものですか。(What is <ANS>'s political situation?)

In the above example, q5 is the first question and q6 is the follow-up question. The question q6 is replaced with q6' using ellipsis handling rules. System replaced "彼 (his)" of q6 with the answer of q5. Because "彼 (his)" refers human and the answer type of q5 is human, and the answer of q5 was the nearest word which suitable to "彼 (his)". But, "彼 (his)" referred "コリン・パウエル (Mr. Colin Powell)" actually. In this case, "コリン・パウエル (Mr. Colin Powell)" was the topic of q5, so "コリン・パウエル (Mr. Colin Powell)" would be better one than the answer of q5. Topic information handling would be implemented in our algorithm.

5 Conclusion

In this paper, we have presented ellipsis handling method for follow-up questions in IAD task. We have classified ellipsis pattern of question sentences into three types and proposed ellipsis handling algorithm for each type. In the evaluation using Formal Run and Reference Run data, there were several cases which our algorithm could not handle ellipsis correctly. According to the analysis of evaluation results, the main reason of low performance was lack of word information for recognition of referential elements. If our system can recognize word meanings correctly, some errors will not occur and ellipsis handling works well.

We have already improved our ellipsis handling method with recognition of target question. In the evaluation of QAC3, our system searches elliptical element in the previous question. However, we have not tested this new algorithm using test correction. In the future work, we will test this algorithm and apply it for other QA application.

References

EDR Home Page. http://www2.nict.go.jp/kk/e416/EDR/J_index.html.

Junichi Fukumoto, Tetsuya Endo, and Tatsuhiro Niwa. 2002. Rits-QA: Ritsumeikan question answering system used for QAC-1. In *Working Notes of the 3rd NTCIR Workshop Meeting: Part IV QAC1*, pages 113–116. National Institute of Informatics.

Junichi Fukumoto, Tatsuhiro Niwa, Makoto Itoigawa, and Megumi Matsuda. 2004. Rits-QA: List answer detection and context task with ellipsis handling. In *Working Notes of the 4th NTCIR Workshop Meeting*, pages 310–314. National Institute of Informatics.

Tsuneaki Kato, Junichi Fukumoto, and Fumito Masui. 2004. Question answering challenge for information access dialogue - overview of NTCIR-4 QAC2 subtask 3. In *Proceesings of the 5th NTCIR Workshop Meeting on Evaluation of Information Access Technologies*, pages 291–297. National Institute of Informatics.

Tsuneaki Kato, Junichi Fukumoto, and Fumito Masui. 2005. An overview of NTCIR-5 QAC3. In *Proceesings of the 5th NTCIR Workshop Meeting on Evaluation of Information Access Technologies*, pages 361–372. National Institute of Informatics.

Megumi Matsuda and Junichi Fukumoto. 2005. Answering questions of IAD task using reference resolution of follow-up questions. In *Proceesings of the 5th NTCIR Workshop Meeting on Evaluation of Information Access Technologies*, pages 414–421. National Institute of Informatics.

Masaki Murata, Masao Utiyama, and Hitoshi Isahara. 2002. A question-answering system using unit estimation and probabilistic near-terms ir. In *Working Notes of NTCIR Workshop 3 Meeting QAC1*, pages 47–54. National Institute of Informatics.

Yutaka Sasaki, Hideki Isozaki, Tsutomu Hirao, Koji Kokuryou, and Eisaku Maeda. 2002. NTT's QA systems for NTCIR QAC-1. In *Working Notes of NTCIR Workshop 3 Meeting QAC1*, pages 63–70. National Institute of Informatics.

User-Centered Evaluation of Interactive Question Answering Systems

Diane Kelly[1], Paul B. Kantor[2], Emile L. Morse[3], Jean Scholtz[3] & Ying Sun[2]

University of North Carolina
Chapel Hill, NC 27599
dianek@email.unc.edu

Rutgers University
New Brunswick, NJ 08901
kantor@scils.rutgers.edu
ysun@scils.rutgers.edu

National Institute of Standards & Technology
Gaithersburg, MD
emile.morse@nist.gov
jean.scholtz@nist.gov

Abstract

We describe a large-scale evaluation of four interactive question answering system with real users. The purpose of the evaluation was to develop evaluation methods and metrics for interactive QA systems. We present our evaluation method as a case study, and discuss the design and administration of the evaluation components and the effectiveness of several evaluation techniques with respect to their validity and discriminatory power. Our goal is to provide a roadmap to others for conducting evaluations of their own systems, and to put forward a research agenda for interactive QA evaluation.

1 Introduction

There is substantial literature on the evaluation of systems in the context of real users and/or realistic problems. The overall design issues were presented by Tague-Sutcliffe (1992) in a classic paper. Other authors who have contributed substantially to the discussion include Hersh and Over (2001). The basic change in viewpoint required, in the study of interactive systems with real users, is that one cannot follow the Cranfield Model, in which specific items (whether documents, or snippets of information) are known to be "good," so that measures can be based on the count of such items (e.g., precision and recall). Instead, one must develop methods and metrics that are sensitive to individual users, tasks and contexts, and robust enough to allow for valid and reliable comparisons across systems.

Most evaluations of QA systems have been conducted as part of the QA Track at TREC. They are system-oriented rather than user-oriented, with a focus on evaluating techniques for answer extraction, rather than interaction and use (Voorhees, 2003). In this paper, we consider an *interactive* system to be a system that supports at least one exchange between the user and system. Further, an interactive system is a system that allows the user full or partial control over content and action.

While factoid QA plays a role in analytical QA, analytical QA also includes other activities, such as comparison and synthesis, and demands much richer interactions between the system, the information, and the user. Thus different evaluation measures are needed for analytical QA systems than for those supporting factoid QA. Emerging work in the QA community is addressing user interaction with factoid-based QA systems and other more complex QA tasks (Diekema, et al., 2004; Liddy, et al., 2004), but developing robust evaluation methods and metrics for interactive, analytical QA systems in realistic settings with target users and tasks remains an unresolved research problem.

We describe a large-scale evaluation of four interactive QA systems with target users, completing target tasks. Here we present the evaluation method and design decisions for each aspect of the study as a case study. The goal of this paper is to identify key issues in the design of evaluations of interactive QA systems and help others construct their own evaluations. While systems participating in this evaluation received individual feedback about the performances of their systems, the purpose of the project was not to compare a series of systems and declare a 'winner.' In this paper we focus on the method and results of that method, rather than the performance of any one system.

In section 2, we describe our evaluation approach, the evaluation environment, systems studied, subjects, corpus and scenarios, and

Proceedings of the Interactive Question Answering Workshop at HLT-NAACL 2006, pages 49–56,
New York City, NY, USA. June 2006.

experimental design. In Section 3 we report our instruments and other data collection techniques. In Section 4 we discuss our evaluation methods, and present key findings regarding the effectiveness of the various evaluation techniques. We conclude by considering future research directions for interactive QA evaluation.

2 Evaluation Approach

This evaluation was conducted as a two-week workshop. The workshop mode gives analysts an opportunity to fully interact with all four systems, complete time-intensive tasks similar to their normal work tasks and lets us evaluate a range of methods and metrics.

The researchers spent approximately 3 weeks onsite preparing and administering the workshop. Intelligence analysts, the study participants, spent 2 weeks onsite. The evaluation employed 8 analysts, 8 scenarios in the chemical/biological WMD domain, and 4 systems – 3 QA systems and a Google[1] baseline system. Each analyst used each system to analyze 2 scenarios and wrote a pseudo-report containing enough structure and content for it to be judged by peer analysts.

During the planning stage, we generated hypotheses about interactive QA systems to guide development of methods and metrics for measuring system effectiveness. Fifteen hypotheses were selected, of which 13 were operationalized. Example hypotheses are presented in Table 1.

A good interactive QA system should …	
1	Support information gathering with lower cognitive workload
2	Assist analysts in exploring more paths/hypotheses
3	Enable analysts to produce higher quality reports
4	Provide useful suggestions to the analyst
5	Provide analysts with more good surprises than bad

Table 1: Example hypotheses

2.1 Evaluation Environment

The experiment was done at the Pacific Northwest National Laboratory (PNNL) in Richland, WA. We used one room with support servers, four rooms with two copies of one system in each and a conference room seating 20, for general meetings, focus group discussions, meetings among observers, meetings among developers, etc.

2.2 QA Systems

Three end-to-end interactive QA systems and a Google baseline were used. System developers were assigned a room, and installed their systems on two workstations in the room.

Before analysts used each system, they were trained by the system developer. Training included a skills check test, and free experimentation. Methods of training included: a script with trainees reproducing steps on their own workstations, a slide presentation with scripted activities, a presentation from a printed manual, and a presentation, orally and with participation, guided by a checklist.

The workstations used during the experiment were Dell workstations configured with Windows XP Professional with updated OS, Intel Pentium IV processor 3.40 Ghz 512 K/800 Mhz, 2 GB DDR 400 SD RAM, 120 GB SATA 7200 RPM hard drive with Data Burst Cache, video card, floppy drive, 16 DVD ROM, and 48/32/48 CDRW.

2.3 Subjects

Analysts who participated in the study were volunteers serving their yearly two-week service requirement as U.S. Naval Reservists. Analysts were recruited by email solicitation of a large pool of potential volunteers. The first 8 positive responders were inducted into the study.

We collected the following data from analysts: age, education level, job type, number of years in the military, number of years conducting analysis work, computer usage, computer expertise, and experience with querying systems. Data about analysts characterizes them on several dimensions. With small samples, this step is critical, but it is also important in studies with larger samples. This type of data lets us describe participants in published reports and ask whether individual differences affect study results. For instance, one might look for a relationship between computer experience and performance.

2.4 Scenarios

Scenarios were developed by a team of analysts from the Air Force Rome Research Lab, and were

[1] Any mention of commercial products or companies is for information only and does not imply recommendation or endorsement by NIST.

vetted to produce 14 appropriate to the collection and target participants. We found after the first two scenarios that while scenario descriptions were sufficient in describing the content of the task, important information regarding context of the description and the format of the report, such as customer and length, was lacking. This omission generated ambiguity in report creation, and caused some uncertainty for the analysts on how to proceed with the task. Thereafter, analysts met as a group in the conference room to agree on additional specifications for each scenario when it was assigned. In addition to this information, the project director and one analyst worked together to design a template for the report, which established a uniform report structure, and specified formatting guidelines such as headings and length. An example scenario is displayed in Figure 1.

Scenario B: [country] Chemical Weapons Program

Before a U.S. military presence is reestablished in [country], a current, thorough study of [country] chemical weapons program must be developed. Your task is to produce a report for the Secretary of the United States Navy regarding general information on [country] and the production of chemical weapons. Provide information regarding [country] access to chemical weapons research, their current capabilities to use and deploy chemical weapons, reported stockpiles, potential development for the next few years, any assistance they have received for their chemical weapons program, and the impact that this information will have on the United States. Please add any other related information to your report.

Customer: Secretary of U.S. Navy
Role: Country desk – [country]
What they want: General report on [country] and CW production

Figure 1. Example Scenario

2.5 Corpus

Using the live Web would make it impossible to replicate the experiment, so we started with the AQUAINT corpus from the Center for Non-Proliferation Studies (CNS). The CNS data consists of the January 2004 distribution of the Eye on Proliferation CD, which has been "disaggregated" by CNS into about 40,000 documents. Once the initial 14 scenarios were delivered to NIST, they were characterized with respect to how well the CNS corpus could support them. Several scenarios had less than 100 documents in the CNS corpus, so to increase the number of documents available for each scenario we supplemented the corpus by mining the Web.

Documents were collected from the Web by semi-automated querying of Google and manual retrieval of the documents listed in the results. A few unusually large and useless items, like CD images, pornography and word lists, were deleted. The approximate counts of different kinds of files, as determined by their file extensions, are summarized in Table 2.

Source	All Files	Documents	Images
CNS	40192	39932	945
Other	261590	48035	188729

Table 2: Characteristics of corpus in bytes

2.6 Experimental Design

The evaluation workshop included four, two-day blocks. In each block, a pair of analysts was assigned to each room, and a single observer was assigned to the pair of analysts. Analysts used the two machines in each room to work independently during the block. After each block, analysts and observers rotated to different system rooms, so that analysts were paired together only once and observers observed different analysts during each block. The goal in using designed experiments is to minimize the second-order interactions, so that estimates of the main effects can be obtained from a much smaller set of observations than is required for a full factorial design. For instance, one might imagine potential interaction effects of system and scenario (some systems might be better for certain scenarios); system and analysts (some analysts might adapt more quickly to a system); and analyst and scenario (some analysts might be more expert for certain scenarios). To control these potential interactions, we used a modified Greco-Latin 4x4 design.

This design ensured that each analyst was observed by each of the four observers, and used each of the four systems. This design also ensured that each system was, for some analyst, the first, second, third or last to be encountered, and that no analyst did the same pair of scenarios twice. Analyst pairings were unique across blocks. Following standard practice, analysts and scenarios were randomly assigned codenames (e.g. A1, and Scenario A), and systems were randomly assigned to the rows of Table 3. Although observers were simply rotated across the system rows, the assignment of human individuals to code number was random.

Dates	Day 1 2	Day 3 4	Day 5 6	Day 7 8
Scenarios	A, B	C, D	E, F	G, H
System 1	O1	O2	O3	O4
	A1	A2	A3	A4
	A5	A6	A7	A8
System 2	O2	O1	O4	O3
	A4	A3	A2	A1
	A7	A8	A5	A6
System 3	O3	O4	O1	O2
	A2	A1	A4	A3
	A8	A7	A6	A5
System 4	O4	O3	O2	O1
	A3	A4	A1	A2
	A6	A5	A8	A7

Table 3. Experimental design (O=observer; A=analyst)

3 Data Collection

System logs and Glass Box (Hampson & Crowley, 2005) were the core logging methods providing process data. Post-scenario, post-session, post-system and cognitive workload questionnaires, interviews, focus groups, and other user-centered methods were applied to understand more about analysts' experiences and attitudes. Finally, cross-evaluation (Sun & Kantor, 2006) was the primary method for evaluating reports produced.

Each experimental block had two sessions, corresponding to the two unique scenarios. Methods and instruments described below were either administered throughout the experimental block (e.g., observation and logging); at the end of the session, in which case the analyst would complete two of these instruments during the block (e.g., a post-session questionnaire for each scenario); or once, at the end of the experimental block (e.g., a post-system questionnaire). We added several data collection efforts at the end of the workshop to understand more about analysts' overall experiences and to learn more about the study method.

3.1 Observation

Throughout the experimental sessions, trained observers monitored analysts' interactions with systems. Observers were stationed behind analysts, to be minimally intrusive and to allow for an optimal viewing position. Observers used an Observation Worksheet to record activities and behaviors that were expected to be indicative of analysts' level of comfort, and feelings of satisfaction or dissatisfaction. Observers noted analysts' apparent patterns of activities. Finally, observers used the Worksheet to note behaviors about which to follow-up during subsequent session interviews.

3.2 Spontaneous Self-Reports

During the evaluation, we were interested in obtaining feedback from analyst in situ. Analysts were asked to report their experiences spontaneously during the experimental session in three ways: commenting into lapel microphones, using the "SmiFro Console" (described more fully below), and completing a three-item online Status Questionnaire at 30 minute intervals.

The SmiFro Console provided analysts with a persistent tool for commenting on their experiences using the system. It was rendered in a small display window, and analysts were asked to leave this window open on their desktops at all times. It displayed smile and frown faces, which analysts could select using radio buttons. The Console also displayed a text box, in which analysts could write additional comments. The goal in using smiles and frowns was to create a simple, recognizable, and quick way for analysts to provide feedback.

The SmiFro Console contained links to the Status Questionnaires which were designed to solicit analysts' opinions and feedback about the progress of their work during the session. Each questionnaire contained the same three questions, which were worded differently to reflect different moments in time. There were four Status Questionnaires, corresponding to 30-minute intervals during the session: 30, 60, 90, 120 minutes.

3.3 NASA TLX Questionnaire

After completing each scenario, analysts completed the NASA Task Load Index (TLX)[2]. The NASA TLX is a standard instrument used in aviation research to assess pilot workload and was used in this study to assess analysts' subjective cognitive workloads while completing each scenario. The NASA TLX assesses six factors:

[2] http://www.nrl.navy.mil/aic/ide/NASATLX.php

1. *Mental demand*: whether this searching task affects a user's attention, brain, and focus.
2. *Physical demand*: whether this searching task affects a user's health, makes a user tired, etc.
3. *Temporal demand*: whether this searching task takes a lot of time that can't be afforded.
4. *Performance*: whether this searching task is heavy or light in terms of workload.
5. *Frustration*: whether this searching task makes a user unhappy or frustrated.
6. *Effort*: whether a user has spent a lot of effort on this searching task.

3.4 Post-Scenario Questionnaire

Following the NASA TLX, analysts completed the six-item Scenario Questionnaire. This Questionnaire was used to assess dimensions of scenarios, such as their realism and difficulty.

3.5 Post-Session Questionnaire

After completing the Post-Scenario Questionnaire, analysts completed the fifteen-item Post-Session Questionnaire. This Questionnaire was used to assess analysts' experiences using this particular system to prepare a pseudo-report. Each question was mapped to one or more of our research hypotheses. Observers examined these responses and used them to construct follow-up questions for subsequent Post-Session Interviews.

3.6 Post-Session Interview

Observers used a Post-Session Interview Schedule to privately interview each analyst. The Interview Schedule contained instructions to the observer for conducting the interview, and also provided a list of seven open-ended questions. One of these questions required the observer to use notes from the Observation Worksheet, while two called for the observer to use analysts' responses to Post-Session Questionnaire items.

3.7 NASA TLX Weighting Instrument

After using the system to complete two scenarios, analysts completed the NASA-TLX Weighting instrument. The NASA-TLX Weighting instrument was used to elicit a ranking from analysts about the factors that were probed with the NASA-TLX instrument. There are 15 pair-wise comparisons of 6 factors and analysts were forced to choose one in each pair as more important. A simple sum of "wins" is used to assign a weight to each dimension, for the specific analyst.

3.8 Post-System Questionnaire

After the NASA-TLX Weighting instrument, analysts completed a thirty-three item Post-System Questionnaire, to assess their experiences using the specific system used during the block. As with the Post-Session Questionnaire, each question from this questionnaire was mapped to one or more of our research hypotheses and observers asked follow-up questions about analysts' responses to select questions during the Post-System Interview.

3.9 Post-System Interview

Observers used a Post-System Interview Schedule to privately interview each analyst at the end of a block. The Interview Schedule contained instructions to the observer for conducting the interview, as well as six open-ended questions. As in the Post-Session Interview, observers were instructed to construct content for two of these questions from analysts' responses to the Post-System Questionnaire.

3.10 Cross-Evaluation

The last component of each block was Cross Evaluation (Ying & Kantor, 2006). Each analyst reviewed (using a paper copy) all seven reports prepared for each scenario in the block (14 total reports). Analysts used an online tool to rate each report according to 7 criteria using 5-point scales. After analysts completed independent ratings of each report according to the 7 criteria, they were asked to sort the stack of reports into rank order, placing the best report at the top of the pile. Analysts were then asked to use a pen to write the appropriate rank number at the top of each report, and to use an online tool to enter their report rankings. The criteria that the analysts used for evaluating reports were: (1) covers the important ground; (2) avoids the irrelevant materials; (3) avoids redundant information; (4) includes selective information; (5) is well organized; (6) reads clearly and easily; and (7) overall rating.

3.11 Cross-Evaluation Focus Groups

After the Cross Evaluation, focus groups of four

analysts were formed to discuss the results of the Cross Evaluation. These focus groups had two purposes: to develop a consensus ranking of the seven reports for each scenario, and to elicit the aspects, or dimensions, which led each analyst to rank a report high or low in overall quality. These discussions were taped and an observer took notes during the discussion.

3.12 System Logs and Glass Box

Throughout much of the evaluation, logging and Glass Box software captured analysts' interactions with systems. The Glass Box software supports capture of analyst workstation activities including keyboard/mouse data, window events, file open and save events, copy/paste events, and web browser activity. The Glass Box uses a relational database to store time-stamped events and a hierarchical file store where files and the content of web pages are stored. The Glass Box copies every file the analyst opens so that there is a complete record of the evolution of documents. Material on every web page analysts visit is explicitly stored so that each web page can be later recreated by researchers as it existed at the time it was accessed by analysts; screen and audio capture are also available.

The data captured by the Glass Box provides details about analysts' interaction with Microsoft desktop components, such as MS Office and Internet Explorer. User interaction with applications that do not run in a browser and Java applications that may run in a browser are opaque to Glass Box. Although limited information, e.g. Window Title, application name, information copied to the system Clipboard, is captured, the quantity and quality of the data is not sufficient to serve as a complete log of user-system interaction. Thus, a set of logging requirements was developed and implement by each system. These included: time stamp; set of documents the user copied text from; number of documents viewed; number of documents that the system said contained the answer; and analyst's query/question.

3.13 End-of-Workshop Activities

On the final day of the workshop, analysts completed a Scenario Difficulty Assessment task, provided feedback to system developers and participated in two focus group interviews. As part of the Scenario Difficulty Assessment, analysts rated each scenario on 12 dimensions, and also rank-ordered the scenarios according to level of difficulty. After the Scenario Difficulty Assessment, analysts visited each of the three experimental system developers in turn, for a 40-minute free form discussion to provide feedback about systems. As the last event in the workshop, analysts participated in two focus groups. The first was to obtain additional feedback about analysts' overall experiences and the second was to obtain feedback from analysts about the evaluation process.

4 Discussion

In this section, we present key findings with regard to the effectiveness of these data collection techniques in discriminating between systems.

Corpus. The corpus consisted of a specialized collection of CNS and Web documents. Although this combination resulted in a larger, diverse corpus, this corpus was not identical to the kinds of corpora analysts use in their daily jobs. In particular, analysts search corpora of confidential government documents. Obviously, these corpora are not readily available for QA system evaluation. Thus, creation of a realistic corpus with documents that analysts are used to is a significant challenge.

Scenarios. Scenarios were developed by two consultants from the Rome AFRL. The development of appropriate and robust scenarios that mimicked real-world tasks was a time intensive process. As noted earlier, we discovered that in spite of this process, scenarios were still missing important contextual details that govern report generation. Thus, creating scenarios involves more than identifying the content and scope of the information sought. It also requires identifying information such as customer, role and deadline.

Analysts. Analysts in this experiment were naval reservists, recruited by email solicitation of a large pool of potential volunteers; the first 8 positive responders were inducted into the study. Such self-selection is virtually certain to produce a non-random sample. However, this sample was from the target population which adds to the validity of the findings. We recommend that decision makers evaluating systems expend substantial effort to recruit analysts typical of those who will be using the system and be aware that self selection biases are likely to be present. Care should be taken to ensure that subjects have a working knowledge of basic tasks and systems, such as using browsers, Microsoft Word, and possibly Microsoft Excel.

Experimental Design. We used a great deal of randomization in our experimental design; the purpose was to obtain more valid statistical results. All statistical results are conditioned by the statement "if the analysts and tasks used are a random sample from the universe of relevant analysts and tasks." Scenarios were not a random selection among possible scenarios; instead, they were tailored to the corpus. Similarly, analysts were not a random sample of all possible analysts, since they were in fact self-selected from a smaller pool of all possible analysts. The randomization in the experimental rotation allowed us to mitigate biases introduced by non-probability sampling techniques across system, as well as curtail any potential bias introduced by observers.

Data Collection. We employed a wide variety of data collection techniques. Key findings with respect to each technique are presented below.

Questionnaires were powerful discriminators across the range of hypotheses tested. They were also relatively economical to develop and analyze. Most analysts were comfortable completing questionnaires, although with eight repetitions they sometimes became fatigued. Questionnaires also provided a useful opportunity to check the validity of experimental materials such as scenarios.

The NASA TLX was sensitive in assessing analysts' workloads for each scenario. It was cheap to administer and analyze, and has established validity and reliability as an instrument in a different arena, where there are real time pressures to control a mechanical system.

Formative techniques, such as interviews and focus groups, provided the most useful feedback, especially to system developers. Interview and focus group data usually provide researchers with important information that supplements, qualifies or elaborates data obtained through questionnaires. With questionnaires, users are forced to quantify their attitudes using numeric values. Data collection methods designed to gather qualitative data, such as interviews, provide users with opportunities to elaborate and qualify their attitudes and opinions. One effective technique used in this evaluation was to ask analysts to elaborate on some of their numeric ratings from questionnaires. This allows us to understand more about why analysts used particular values to describe their attitudes and experiences. It is important to note that analysis of qualitative data is costly – interviews were transcribed and training is needed to analyze and interpret data. Training is also necessary to conduct such interviews. Because researchers are essentially the 'instrument' it is important to learn to moderate one's own beliefs and behaviors while interviewing. It is particularly important that interviewers not be seen by their interviewees as "invested in" any particular system; having individuals who are not system developers conduct interviews is essential.

The SmiFro Console was not effective as implemented. Capturing analysts' *in situ* thoughts with minimal disruption remains a challenge. Although SmiFro Console was not particularly effective, status report data was easy to obtain and somewhat effective, but defied analysis.

Cross evaluation of reports was a sensitive and reliable method for evaluating product. Complementing questionnaires, it is a good method for assessing the *quality of the analysts' work products*. The method is somewhat costly in terms of analysts' time (contributing approximately 8% of the total time required from subjects), and analysis requires skill in statistical methods.

System logs answered several questions not addressable with other methods including the Glass Box. However, logging is expensive, rarely reusable, and often unruly when extracting particular measures. Development of a standard logging format for interactive QA systems is advisable. The Glass Box provided data on user interaction across all systems at various levels of granularity. The cost of collection is low but the cost of analysis is probably prohibitive in most cases. NIST's previous experience using Glass Box allowed for more rapid extraction, analysis and interpretation of data, which remained a very time consuming and laborious process. Other commercial tools are available that capture some of the same data and we recommend that research teams evaluate such tools for their own evaluations.

Hypotheses. We started this study with hypotheses about the types of interactions that a good QA system should support. Of course, different methods were more or less appropriate for assessing different hypotheses. Table 4 displays part of our results with respect to the example hypotheses presented above in Table 1. For each of the example hypotheses provided in Table 1, we show which method was used.

	Ques.	NASA TLX	Smi-Fro	Cross-Eval.	Logs	Glass Box
1		X			X	X
2	X					
3	X			X		
4	X				X	X
5	X		X			

Table 4: Most effective methods for gathering data about example hypotheses (see Table 1).

Although not reported here, we note that the performance of each of the systems evaluated in this study varied according to hypothesis; in particular, some systems did well according to some hypotheses and poor according to others.

Interaction. Finally, while the purposes of this paper were to present our evaluation method for interactive question answering systems, our instruments elicited interesting results about analysts' perceptions of interaction. Foremost among them, users of interactive systems *expect systems to exhibit behaviors which can be characterized as understanding what the user is looking for, what the user has done and what the user knows.* Analysts in this study expected interactive systems to track their actions over time, both with the system and with information.

5 Conclusions

We have sketched a method for evaluating interactive analytic question answering system, identified key design decisions that developers must make in conducting their own evaluations, and described the effectiveness of some of our methods. Clearly, each evaluation situation is different, and it is difficult to develop one-size-fits-all evaluation strategies, especially for interactive systems. However, there are many opportunities for developing shared frameworks and an infrastructure for evaluation. In particular, the development of scenarios and corpora are expensive and should be shared. The creation of sharable questionnaires and other instruments that are customizable to individual systems can also contribute to an infrastructure for interactive QA evaluation.

We believe that important opportunities exist through interactive QA evaluation for understanding more about the interactive QA process and developing extensive theoretical and empirical foundations for research. We encourage system developers to think beyond independent system evaluation for narrow purposes, and conduct evaluations that create and inform theoretical and empirical foundations for interactive question answering research that will outlive individual systems. Although we do not have space here to detail the templates, instruments, and analytical schemas used in this study, we hope that the methods and metrics developed in connection with our study are a first step in this direction[3]. We plan to publish the full set of results from this study in the future.

References

Diekema, A. R., Yilmazel, O., Chen, J., Harwell, S., He, L., & Liddy, E. D. (2004). Finding answers to complex questions. In M. T. Maybury's, *New directions in question answering*. MIT Press, MA., 141-152.

Hampson, E., & Crowley, P. (2005). Instrumenting the intelligence analysis process. *Proceedings of the 2005 International Conference on Intelligence Analysis*, McLean, VA.

Hersh, W. & Over, P. (2001). Introduction to a special issue on interactivity at the Text Retrieval Conference (TREC). *Information Processing & Management 37*(3), 365-367.

Liddy, E. D., Diekema, A. R., & Yilmazel, O. (2004). Context-based question-answering evaluation. *Proceedings of SIGIR '04*, Sheffield, UK, 508-509.

Sun, Y., & Kantor, P. (2006). Cross-evaluation: A new model for information system evaluation. *Journal of American Society for Information Science & Technology*.

Tague-Sutcliffe, J. (1992). The pragmatics of information retrieval experimentation, revisted. *Information Processing & Management, 28*(4), 467-490.

Voorhees, E. M. (2003). Evaluating the evaluation: A case study using the TREC 2002 Question Answering Task. *Proceedings of HLT-NAACL'03*, 181-188.

[3] The NIST team maintains a password-protected website (http://control.nist.gov/amc/) for materials related to this project. Send email to emile.morse@nist.gov.

Association for Computational Linguistics
209 N. Eighth Street
Stroudsburg, Pennsylvania 18360

Workshop on Computationally Hard Problems and Joint Inference in Speech and Language Processing 2006

Held at HLT/NAACL 2006

New York, New York, USA
9 June 2006

ISBN: 978-1-61738-494-3